Augsburg
Sermons for
Children

Gospels, Series C

Augsburg
Sermons for
Children

Augsburg
MINNEAPOLIS

AUGSBURG SERMONS FOR CHILDREN
Gospels, Series C

Interior design: Virginia Aretz, Northwestern Printcrafters
Cover design: Lecy Design

Library of Congress Cataloging-in-Publication Data
(Revised for vol. 3)

Augsburg sermons for children.
    Includes bibliographical references.
    Contents: [1] Gospels, series A—[2] Gospels,
series B—[3] Gospels, series C.
    1. Bible. N.T. Gospels—Children's sermons.
    2. Lutheran Church—Sermons.   3. Church year sermons.
    4. Sermons, American.   I. Augsburg Fortress (Publisher)
    BS2555.4.A945 1992   252'.53   92-27959
    ISBN 0-8066-2621-6 (v. 1 : alk. paper)
    ISBN 0-8066-2622-4 (v. 2 : alk. paper)
    ISBN 0-8066-2623-2 (v. 3 : alk. paper)

Manufactured in the U.S.A.   AF 9–2623

98   97   96   95   94   1   2   3   4   5   6   7   8   9   10

Contents

———————————————•———————————————

The Rev. Norbert F. Hahn
Grace Lutheran Church
Carrollton, Georgia

The Rev. Marsha C. Anderson
Prince of Peace
Oklahoma City, Oklahoma

Gail Wettstein
Staff Attorney, Oklahoma Court of Criminal Appeals
Oklahoma City, Oklahoma

The Rev. Philip Formo

Preface

—————•—————

When Jesus' disciples tried to prevent parents from bringing their children to him, Jesus stopped the disciples and told them to let the children come to him. He included children in his ministry.

Sometimes the church has done little to include children in its worship services. Now many pastors and church leaders are exploring a number of ways for children to participate, and the children's sermon has great potential.[1] During this special time, the gospel can be communicated to children in ways particularly appropriate for them, taking seriously children's concerns, level of understanding, and interests. Children are full members in the household of faith, and nothing is more important than sowing the seeds of the gospel early in life.

The goal of this book is to present children's sermons through which children can begin to realize the immensity of God's love for them and God's acceptance of them as they are. Even though the messages and activities use simple language and basic concepts, the gospel is not trivialized. The writers of these children's sermons hope that the children will experience God's love and feel the joy that such good news brings.

The introductory material for each of the sermons provides helpful information for using them. After the name of the Sunday and the Gospel text, there are three headings: Focus, Experience, and Preparation. The focus statement encapsulates the theme, the experience statement tells what activity is planned, and the preparations statement describes what needs to be done ahead of time. Though adaptations can be made, these keys for effective use provide basic information about the writers' intentions.

Because "doing" is as important as "talking" with children, many of the children's sermons in this book are designed to encourage active participation as well as conversation with the children. The emphasis is on all levels of being; not just what they might think about (the intellectual), but also how they feel about relationships, experiences, and discoveries (the affective).

———————————

1. *Including Children in Worship* by Elizabeth J. Sandell is an excellent resource that gives many practical ideas beyond children's sermons (Augsburg, Minneapolis).

Some of the children's sermons use objects, props, or special arrangements, but these sermons are not like some object lessons that ask children to make symbolic connections between an object and a spiritual concept. Such abstract thinking is beyond most children's ability. Objects and props in these sermons are on a level children can understand.

If an object or prop is part of a children's sermon, let the children hold it and handle it when that is possible. They will learn more from their own experience than from simply watching you. Asking a couple children to help you open a backpack or hold a posterboard helps them feel needed and important.

As you plan to present these children's sermons, you will bring your own style and gifts to your time with the children. Your gifts of spontaneity, flexibility, and creativity will give life to the messages. Children are usually eager to join in the experiences you lead, and your enthusiasm will help them gain much from your time together.

Your primary audience will be the children who come forward to participate, but other children who are too hesitant or shy to come up, as well as adults and youth, will also be listening and watching. When you ask the children questions, all the people in the congregation will be listening and probably answering to themselves.

The congregation may respond to the dialogue that is part of the children's sermons with warm, affirming laughter. This is usually not disruptive but rather extends the dialogue and lets you know the congregation is listening. There can be a temptation to play to this larger audience, but do not give in to it. The children will sense that they are no longer your primary focus, and you will break the essential bond you have been developing with them.

Effective dialogue develops with good questions and responses. Open questions such as "What do you do when you know a storm is coming?" generate interesting responses. Because you do not suggest a particular answer, you are more likely to get authentic and sometimes unexpected responses. Closed questions, ones that can be answered with yes or no or a brief, factual answer rarely lead to further conversation. Yet some closed questions are helpful to define words or to identify a person or action. For example, "What was Jesus doing when the storm came up?" (Luke 8:22-25) can be answered, "He was sleeping." Following that with open questions will involve the children more fully.

Children's sermons that are more grace oriented than law oriented convey God's love more clearly. As much as possible, messages to children should communicate how God shows grace through Jesus Christ; how God has worked through the lives of people in Bible times, throughout the ages, and today; and how God loves each of the children very much.[2]

---

2. Special thanks to Lisa Stafford and Gail Wettstein, who contributed to *Augsburg Sermons for Children, Gospels, Series A*, for providing some of the material used in this preface. (Gail also contributed to this Series C volume.)

First Sunday in Advent
——————————•——————————

The Gospel: Luke 21:25-36

Focus: Advent is a time to remember whose birthday we celebrate at Christmas.

Experience: You and the children will talk about the ways we try to remember something.

Preparation: Bring an appointment calendar, pieces of string, a message pad or refrigerator message board with *milk* and *crackers* written on one of the slips. Prepare a simple Advent calendar, photocopy it, and bring copies for each child. Each day should have a suggested prayer, Bible verse, or activity. Here are some suggestions.

Advent Calendar Ideas

– Say a prayer asking God to help us remember that Christmas is Jesus' birthday.
– Read John 3:16 and talk to someone in your family about it.
– Tell someone your favorite Christmas memory.
– Play a recording of "Silent Night" or sing it.
– Memorize the first stanza of "Silent Night" and sing it.
– Using white paper bakery bags, sand, and votive candles, make luminaries for a walkway or driveway (if not possible, find and display a candle or a decoration that reminds you of light).
– Draw a couple of Christmas symbols such as a star, an angel, or a Christmas tree, then color them and cut them out.
– Do something nice for someone and try to keep it a secret.
– Read Micah 5:2 and notice the city that is named there.
– Say a prayer asking God to bless everyone in your family and your friends during this special time.
– Make a Jesse tree. Put a small branch in a can of sand and hang items and cutouts that remind you of Jesus.
– Read Isaiah 9:6-7.
– Make some Christmas cards and give or mail them to someone (maybe Grandma and Grandpa).
– Pray for people who don't have what they need (food, a home).

- Give some money or a gift to your church or a group that helps other people who don't have what they need.
- Read Isaiah 11:1-3.
- Play a recording of "Away in a Manger" or sing it.
- Memorize the first stanza of "Away in a Manger" and sing it.
- Put up some Christmas decorations in your room or by your bed.
- Tell someone what your favorite Christmas decoration is.
- With others in your family, talk about this question: How will our neighbors know we are celebrating Jesus' birthday and not just Christmas in general?
- Play a recording of "O Little Town of Bethlehem" or sing it.
- Memorize the first stanza of "O Little Town of Bethlehem" and sing it.
- Read one of your favorite Christmas stories or books.
- Call or visit someone to let that person know you are thinking of him or her as Christmas comes near.
- Put out some seeds or cereal for the birds to eat.
- With some friends, act out the story of Jesus' birth, or use figures from a creche to act it out. See Luke 2:1-20.
- Memorize Luke 2:11 and say it to someone in your family.
- Make Christmas cookies (if not possible, make a Christmas decoration out of old Christmas cards or colored paper).
- Read Matthew 2:1-11 and act out the story of the wise men with some friends.

Remember

Has anyone ever told you something like this, "Now remember to take out the garbage," or "Remember to pick up your toys," or "Remember to turn out the light"? (*Allow time for responses.*) Sometimes Mom or Dad or someone else will try to remind us of something we are to do. There are other ways we might be reminded of something we need to remember.

(*Open appointment calendar*) On my appointment calendar I have written the places I need to be this coming week. The calendar reminds me of what I need to do.

Years ago people used to say that if you need to remember something, you should tie a string around your finger. Is there anyone here who needs to remember something today? (*Ask what they need to remember and then tie strings around fingers.*) On the refrigerator door at home we have a pad like this. (*Hold up the message pad.*) Anyone in the family can write a note on it to remind us of somewhere we need to be or something we need to buy. Can anyone read this? (*Wait for someone to read it.*) That's right, we are out of milk and crackers.

There are many ways for us to be reminded. This morning we begin a season of the year that is only four weeks long. Does anyone know what we call this season? (*Older children might know.*) It is called Advent. Advent means something is coming. Our job during Advent is to remember *what* is coming. It is much more important than remembering to buy milk or crackers.

Can anyone tell me whose birthday we will be celebrating in just over four weeks? (*Responses.*) Jesus' birthday. With all the shopping and baking and tree trimming we could forget whose birthday we are going to celebrate.

I have something for each of you that can remind you of whose birthday we are going to celebrate. What does this look like? (*Responses.*) That's right, it is a calendar—it's an Advent calendar. We start with today, and we follow the days all the way to Christmas. On each of the days there is a suggestion for you to read a Bible verse, thank Jesus for something special, or do something. After you have done the suggestion for the day, draw an X through it. Then you can see that Christmas is coming closer. Each day you will be reminded of ways we can celebrate Jesus' birthday. With this calendar, you won't need a string on your finger or a message pad.

For today, the first Sunday in Advent, the calendar tells us to ask God to help us remember that Christmas is Jesus' birthday. So let's do that. Let's close our eyes and fold our hands and pray.

"Dear God, we look forward to Christmas. Help us to remember that it is Jesus' birthday. Thank you for sending Jesus and for loving us. Help each of us to show our love for you in the way we treat others. Amen." As you go back, be sure you each have an Advent calendar.   **—P.F.**

Second Sunday in Advent
————————————— • —————————————

The Gospel: Luke 3:1-6

Focus: John the Baptist reminds us that it is necessary to prepare for Christmas. For us, part of our preparation usually includes shopping for gifts, trimming a tree, and preparing special foods.

Experience: The children will compare their preparations and those of John the Baptist.

Preparation: To talk about John the Baptist, you could bring a vest or garment of fake fur, sandals, honey, and a picture or drawing of locusts or grasshoppers. You will need a Christmas decoration, a present, wrapping paper, and tape.

Get Ready

This morning I would like to ask how you get ready for a special event. What did you do to get ready for church this morning? (*Listen for answers that include activities like getting out of bed, eating breakfast, brushing teeth, and getting dressed.*)

At this time of year we are also busy getting ready for another important event. What is it? (*Christmas.*) We are also getting ready for Christmas here at church. Look around and tell me what we have done to get ready. (*Wait for answers regarding a Christmas tree, decorations, advent candles.*) How have you been getting ready at home? (*They might tell you about trimming a tree, wrapping gifts, etc.*)

That reminds me, I have a gift right here for my nephew. (*Say what it is—mittens, a toy, etc., and show them.*) Let's wrap it. Who will help me? (*Wrap the gift.*) Thanks for your help.

That's one way to get ready for Christmas. We get ready by wrapping gifts, trimming a tree, and baking cookies. (*Put present and wrapping away.*)

In our Bible lesson this morning we read about a man who was getting ready for the coming of Jesus. This man had strange clothes and ate strange food. We call him John the Baptist. Who wants to pretend to be John? (*Dress child in fur vest or garment and sandals.*) Now that's what he wore, but this is what he ate. (*Hand the child a bottle of honey and a picture of locusts or grasshoppers.*) Now who can tell me what (*child's name*) is holding? Although he might not have dressed like you or eaten a hamburger, John the Baptist was like you in some ways. He was busy getting ready for Jesus to come. He was telling people to repent, to say they were sorry for what they had done wrong.

We like to go shopping and decorate trees and eat Christmas cookies, but John the Baptist reminds us this morning that we also need to get ready in another way. We need to tell Jesus that we are sorry for our sins. We need to ask Jesus to help us get ready for his birthday.

Let's talk to Jesus. Please fold your hands and close your eyes and we will pray. "Dear Jesus, we want to be ready for Christmas—for your birthday. We are sorry for the times we don't listen to Mom or Dad, for the times we are selfish with our toys. Thank you for forgiving us when we say we are sorry. Thank you for helping us get ready for your birthday. Amen."

That's the way John got ready for Jesus. That's the way we can prepare for Christmas.   **—P.F.**

Third Sunday in Advent

———————————— • ————————————

The Gospel: Luke 3:7-18

Focus: In one form or another Christmas has been mentioned in church for the last two weeks and perhaps the children are getting tired of waiting. We will focus on how difficult it is to wait and the fact that some things are worth the wait.

Experience: The children will hear a story about someone who had a difficult time waiting.

Preparation: Think about your own experience of looking forward to Christmas. If there are objects that help to illustrate the challenge of waiting, use them in your story.

The Waiting Game

(Begin by sitting quietly as if you are "waiting." In silence look around as if you are becoming anxious. Repeatedly look at your watch. Attempt to remain quiet for thirty seconds.)

When I was your age it was very hard for me to wait. At school I didn't like to wait in line for a drink at the fountain. At the park I didn't like to wait for my turn to go down the slide. I just didn't like to wait. For two weeks we have been waiting for Christmas to come, and it's still not here. Do you feel as if you have been waiting a long time for Christmas? *(Responses.)*

Let me tell you a story about a little girl named Sara. Sara was a six-year-old redhead who had been waiting for Christmas. Finally Christmas Eve arrived, but Sara still had a lot of waiting to do. Her uncles, aunts, and cousins, dressed in their Christmas best, would slowly arrive at Sara's house. First Sara would have to wait until the dinner was served and everyone had eaten. After dessert all the dishes would have to be washed. The waiting was still not over. Everyone would gather in the living room to sing Christmas carols. Finally Sara's dad would bring out a Bible, and Sara would have to wait for him to read all twenty verses of the Christmas story from the Gospel of Luke and close with prayer. Then, and only then, could Sara and all her cousins begin to open the presents. Finally Sara's waiting time was over.

Do you open your presents on Christmas Eve like Sara or on Christmas Day? (*Responses.*) What do you have to wait for in your home before you are able to open your presents? (*Responses.*)

Sometimes waiting is an important thing to do. Like Sara, I remember having to wait to open my presents. I don't remember very many of the things that were in those colorfully wrapped boxes, but I still remember waiting.

At Christmastime there is something else we are waiting for. Can you tell me what it is? (*Wait for their answers, and help them to remember Jesus' birth.*) In just one more week we will celebrate Jesus' birthday. Christmas is more than presents and Christmas cookies. We are celebrating God's best present to us, Jesus. God's present to us is really worth the wait.   **—P.F.**

Fourth Sunday in Advent

———————————— • ————————————

The Gospel: Luke 1:39-45 (46-55)

Focus: Just as John, still in Elizabeth's womb, "cheered" for the unborn Jesus, so we will cheer for Jesus on his birthday.

Experience: Children learn quickly what it means to cheer or applaud at a special event. The children will join in a conversation about how we cheer for Jesus when he is born and they will sing a carol.

Preparation: To illustrate what we use for cheering, bring a megaphone (*roll up a large piece of paper into a cone shape*), pom poms, and other objects that might be used for cheering. Choose a Christmas carol or song the children know well. At the end of the sermon they will sing the song together.

Cheers

I brought some special things today. Maybe you can tell me what they are. (*Take out the megaphone.*) Do you know what this is? (*Wait for their answer.*) That's right. It's used by cheerleaders to lead us at a game. (*Take out any other objects you have brought.*) How are these used? (*Responses.*) That's right. They too are used for cheering.

I would like to tell you a story about two cousins. How many of you have cousins? (*Responses.*) Mary and Elizabeth were cousins. They were already grown up, but they were still good friends, just the way they were when they were young.

Early one morning Mary was sleeping. Slowly, as the sun rose, it shone on Mary's house and finally shone right through her window. She woke up and smiled. Today was the day! She was going to visit her cousin Elizabeth. Quickly she got up and put on her nicest clothes. Wanting to be ready for the long walk ahead of her, Mary ate a good breakfast and put on her best sandals.

As the hot sun began to beat down on her, Mary finally arrived at Elizabeth's home. She knocked hard on the large wooden door. When Elizabeth came to answer, she was very happy to see her cousin. As she looked closer at Mary, she realized that Mary too was going to have a baby. Elizabeth was so excited. She felt her baby jump inside of her. Elizabeth felt as if the baby inside of her were cheering for the baby Mary was going to have.

It won't be long now until we too will be cheering for a baby. What baby am I talking about? (*Wait for the answer.*) That's right, baby Jesus, Mary's baby. But you know, we usually don't use megaphones, or pom poms when we cheer for Jesus. Do you have any idea what we might use or how we cheer for Jesus? (*Wait for possible answers.*)

We cheer for Jesus with our voices in a Sunday school program. We cheer for Jesus when we sing Christmas carols like "O Little Town of Bethlehem" or "Joy to the World." We cheer for Jesus when we worship him right here at church. In a few days we will finish getting ready for Christmas, and we will be cheering for Jesus. Let's practice our cheer by singing together one of our favorite Christmas songs. (*Close by singing a favorite carol together. You might want to invite the congregation to sing also.*) **—P.F.**

Christmas Eve

———————————•———————————

The Gospel: Luke 2:1-20

Focus: In the minds of children, Christmas often is synonymous with presents. The purpose of this sermon is to remind children of the greatest present of all.

Experience: The children will talk about the presents they have received in the past and the presents they hope to receive this Christmas. Through dialogue and opening a present, the children will be reminded of God's gift to them.

Preparation: Place in each of three or four boxes a picture of a popular toy. In the largest box place a crèche. Gift wrap each of the boxes, making sure you will know which of the boxes contains the crèche.

The Greatest Present

What are you excited about this time of year? (*Allow children to respond.*)

Do any of you remember what you received for Christmas last year? (*Wait for possible answers.*)

It's easy for us to forget, isn't it?

Is there anything sitting under your tree at home? (*Allow children to answer.*)

I brought along some presents for us to open today. Let's see what they are. (*Ask a child to open the first box.*) What is this? Would anyone like one of these for Christmas? (*Repeat the same dialogue as you invite other children to open the small packages.*)

Now I have a very special present for us to open. Would you please open it for us? (*Let another child open the present containing the crèche.*) What is it? That's right. It is Jesus in a manger. Of all the presents we might receive tonight or tomorrow morning, Jesus is the greatest and best present.

(*Pick up the pictures of the favorite toys.*) We can like our presents very much, but can they like us or love us in return? (*No.*)

Jesus is the only present that we love, and he loves us back. Jesus was born into this world to show God's love for each of us. Of all the presents you will receive this Christmas, remember who the greatest present is. That's right. The greatest present is Jesus.   **—P.F.**

Christmas Day

————————————————— • —————————————————

The Gospel: Luke 2:1-20

Focus: The story of Jesus' birth is the essence of Christmas.

Experience: As the story is told, the children will fill in the missing words.

Preparation: You may wish to write the story out on a large tagboard and leave blanks for the words you want the children to say. Otherwise, practice reading with pauses.

The Greatest Story Ever Told

This morning I am going to tell a story. It's a story that reminds us why we are all here today. (*If your congregation has a Sunday school pageant, you might mention that some of the children have already acted out the story.*)

You have heard the story many times. Yet, like some of your favorite bedtime stories, it's one that you like to hear over and over again. Today you are going to help me tell the story. (*If you have it on tagboard, ask those who can read to follow along.*) Sometimes I will stop and let you say the next word. That means you are going to have to listen very carefully. (*Here is a suggested script.*)

Many years ago the king, Caesar Augustus, told the people they had to return to the town where they were born to pay their taxes. So Joseph left the town of Nazareth and headed toward the town of Bethlehem. He took his wife, whose name was _____ (Mary).

Joseph put her on a _____ (donkey) to ride all the way. It was a difficult journey for Mary because she was expecting a _____ (baby). When they came to the town of _____ (Bethlehem), Mary had her firstborn son and wrapped him in soft cloths and put him in a _____ (manger). There were shepherds in the field keeping watch over their _____ (flocks, sheep). An angel came to them and said "Don't be afraid, I have good news for you. Today in Bethlehem a baby is born and his name is _____ (Jesus, Christ the Lord). You will find him wrapped in soft cloths and lying in a _____ (manger). Suddenly angels appeared in the sky, saying, "Glory to God in the highest and on earth peace to all." Today in Bethlehem is born a Saviour whose name is _____ (Jesus).

Well, that's the story. You really did a great job filling in the words. The most important word is the name of the baby that was born. Let's all say his name again. (*Jesus*) That's the name I want you to remember. **—P.F.**

First Sunday after Christmas

The Gospel: Luke 2:41-52

Focus: The Gospel tells the story of Jesus getting separated from his parents. Whether it was Jesus or his parents who were lost depends upon your perspective.

Experience: You and the children will talk about Jesus' visit to Jerusalem and his encounter with the teachers in the temple.

Preparation: Learn the story printed below. To illustrate being lost, duplicate for each of the children the maze game about the child Jesus in the temple.

Lost and Found

I would like to begin by telling you a story about a twelve-year-old girl named Shelly. One beautiful fall Saturday morning Shelly and her mother decided to walk to a nearby shopping mall. When they arrived, Mom and Shelly decided to each go their own way and meet at the hamburger shop later for lunch.

During the morning Shelly bought jeans in her favorite clothes store, looked at a new CD at the record shop, and dreamed of a new pair of shiny skis in the window of the sports store. Soon she saw some of her friends, and before long they were all playing games at the video arcade.

Meanwhile, her mom was waiting for her at the hamburger shop. After an hour, she began to get worried. She walked through the mall and looked in the stores she thought Shelly might have visited. Shelly's mom felt like she was walking through a maze. Finally she walked home, hoping to find Shelly along the way.

But Shelly wasn't at home either, so Mom returned to the mall with Shelly's older brother and they looked in all Shelly's favorite stores. She was nowhere to be found.

Finally, her brother asked, "Have you tried the video arcade?" Quickly they ran to the arcade. As they approached the door, they found Shelly with her friends. "Where have you been?" her mom asked. "I though you were lost."

"Oh, sorry, Mom, but I met Jenny and Cindy and forgot about the time." Finally they were all together again.

How many of you have ever been lost? (*Allow them to answer.*)
Where were you lost and who found you? (*Allow them to answer.*)
Our Bible story today is about something that happened to Jesus
when he was twelve years old. He was excited to go with his parents to Jerusalem for a special religious holiday. As they walked
toward the temple, from a distance he saw the white stone walls
and the golden roof. There were lots of people in the temple, and
Jesus became separated from his mom and dad.

Thinking Jesus was in the crowd of people from their home
town of Nazareth, Mary and Joseph began to walk home. When
they couldn't find Jesus, they returned to Jerusalem to find their
son. They looked at the inn in which they stayed. They looked in
the streets packed with people from many places. Finally they decided to look one more time in the temple. And, sure enough,
that's where they found him. "Where have you been, Jesus?" they
asked. "We have been worried about you."

Jesus said, "I have been here with the teachers, talking about my
Father in heaven. I haven't been lost."

Sometimes you might be playing down the street and forget to
tell Mom or Dad where you are. You don't think you are lost. The
problem is that Mom or Dad have no idea where to find you. They
are afraid you are lost. When they do find you, they are really
happy. When Mary and Joseph found Jesus talking with the teachers, they didn't understand what Jesus was up to, but they certainly were happy to find him again.

I have a surprise for each of you today. Do you know what a
maze is? (*Allow children to answer.*) It is a game. You begin at one
end and you try to find your way through the twisted path to the
other end. (*Point to the maze.*) You begin here and try to find your
way to the child Jesus in the temple. (*Hand out mazes.*)   **—PF.**

Jesus in the Temple

Luke 2:41-52 tells the story of Jesus as a boy becoming separated from his parents when the family had been in Jerusalem for the festival of the Passover. His parents wanted to leave for home but didn't know where Jesus was. They hunted all over and finally found him with the teachers in the temple. Pretend you are there and that you can help Jesus' parents by finding the right path through this maze.

Second Sunday after Christmas
—————————————————— • ——————————————————

The Gospel: John 1:1-18

Focus: At Christmastime one important messenger is the mail carrier. The important message is printed on many Christmas cards. In our Gospel, John the Baptist was a messenger, and the message was that Jesus was coming. Once Jesus came, we saw the real messenger and the message all wrapped up in one person.

Experience: Through story and illustration the children will be reminded that Jesus is the message of God's love that has come in flesh.

Preparation: Collect some Christmas cards that mention Jesus' birth and some envelopes.

Messages and Messengers

I want to show you something this morning. It is something you have received in the mail during most of December. I have received a lot of these in the mail. What are they? (*Show the Christmas cards and allow children to answer.*) They are all very nice, but some cards are special. (*Show them a couple cards.*)

Who brought these cards to my house? (*Wait for answer.*)

That's right, a mail carrier brought them. Each card might have a different picture on it, but the message is often the same. What is the message on many Christmas cards? (*Allow children to answer.*) That's right. They wish us Merry Christmas. Also, many cards remind us that Jesus was born at Christmas. That's the most important message.

In our Bible lesson for today we read about a messenger. He isn't a mail carrier but a prophet—someone who wants to tell us some important news. His name is John the Baptist. We talked about him a few weeks ago. John the Baptist was that man who wore camel hair skins and sandals and ate honey and grasshoppers. He had a very important job. He was to bring a message to everyone who would listen to him. The message was the same message I found on many of my Christmas cards. What was that message? (*Wait for answers.*) That's right—that Jesus was coming.

I have talked about two messengers. One is the mail carrier. The other is John the Baptist.

But God didn't just send us a messenger to tell us of his love. God sent his Son, Jesus. We have just celebrated his birthday. Christmas cards can be pretty and fun to read, but God sent us something much better than a message. He sent his very own son. That's what we are thankful for today.   **—P.F.**

The Epiphany of Our Lord

———————————————————— • ————————————————————

The Gospel: Matthew 2:1-12

Focus: The Gospel contrasts the king that Herod thought Jesus was with the King the wise men came to find.

Experience: Through the story of the wise men, the children will experience Jesus as the King of love.

Preparation: Gather some of the props used for your pageant or nativity, such as the costumes and gifts the wise men bring.

The King of Love

(*Hold the lectern Bible in front of the children and with reverence open it to Matthew 2. While tracing around the outer edge with your index finger, say,* "This is the Word of God and today we hear about the story of the wise men." *This story is a good one to read out loud to the children. Use your props as you read or tell the story.*)

This is a wonderful story about a star and kings and gifts and a long, difficult journey. The story also has its dark side—the evil and jealous Herod who also happened to be a king.

As I tell the story, will you help me fill in missing parts when I ask you? (*Yes.*) The wise men asked Herod where to find baby Jesus. Herod didn't know, so he asked the wise men to tell him when they found Jesus.

Then off the wise men went to the town where Jesus was born. What was the name of the town? (*Bethlehem.*) They watched something up in the sky which was leading them. What was it? (*A star.*) Yes, a star.

The wise men found Jesus with his mother. What was her name? (*Mary.*) They gave Jesus gifts. But then God warned them in a dream not to go back to Herod, who was a bad man. So what do you think they did? (*Responses. Help them arrive at the answer that they went home a different way.*)

King Herod tried to trick the wise men, but the wise men tricked him instead. They both wanted to find the baby Jesus but for different reasons. If Herod had found Jesus, he was going to kill him. Herod believed that when Jesus became an adult, he would try to take Herod's place as king.

But the wise men came to worship a different kind of king. And we know that they were right and Herod was wrong. Jesus became a King without a throne and without an army. His only weapon was love. He was and is the King who loved little children, who healed the sick, and who invited *everyone* to love as he loved.

I think I understand why the wise men came from so far and risked their lives to find Jesus. They knew that a King of Love would be the the kind of king God would give us.   **—R.J.C.**

The Baptism of Our Lord—First Sunday in Epiphany
— • —

The Gospel: Luke 3:15-17, 21-22

Focus: In being baptized Jesus accepted God's claim on his life.

Experience: The children experience God's claim on their lives and learn to associate it with baptism.

Preparation: You might wish to plan ahead so that this sermon coincides with a baptism. Otherwise, bring the children to the baptismal font to talk to them.

Hand in Hand with God

(*Hold the lectern Bible in front of the children and with reverence open it to Luke 3. Trace around the outer edge with your index finger.*) This is the Word of God and today we hear the story of when Jesus was baptized by John the Baptist.

From the Bible we learn that before Jesus began to preach and teach and heal, he was baptized. I wonder why Jesus had to be baptized. He wasn't a child but a grown adult. And he was more important than John the Baptist. Yet he allowed John to baptize him with water. (*You may wish to pantomime whatever action you use with water when you baptize*).

I think Jesus allowed himself to be baptized because he was saying yes to God—"Yes, God, let your spirit fill me and make me strong to do your will on earth."

How many of you have been baptized? Raise your hands. Some of you know you have been baptized and others aren't so sure. When you were baptized, the minister asked your parents what your Christian name or your first name was. Your first name reminds you that you are a child of God. (*Have them say their first names.*) This is your Christian name, your baptism name.

I like to think of it this way. When you were baptized God reached out and held your hand. (*Reach out and hold the hands of some or all of the children one at a time as you continue.*) After Jesus was baptized, he began to preach and teach and heal. Together he and his Father were beginning to build a kingdom of love, hand in hand. And so it is with you. You and God have joined hands, and together we all will work to build that same kingdom of love at church and at home.

I invite everyone in the congregation to join hands, and together, let us pray:

"We have been baptized with the Holy Spirit and together, hand in hand with God, we will continue to build Jesus' kingdom of love. Amen."   **—R.J.C.**

Second Sunday in Epiphany
—————————————— • ——————————————

The Gospel: John 2:1-22

Focus: Jesus Christ is God's best gift (John 2:10).

Experience: The children will see that the best is saved until last because it is the best.

Preparation: Bring two gifts: one wrapped poorly and the other wrapped in expensive paper. Put something old in the first and something new, perhaps a coloring book, in the second.

Saving the Best Gift for Last

(*Hold the lectern Bible in front of the children and with reverence open it to John 2. While tracing around the outer edge with your index finger, say,* "This is the Word of God, and today we discover what was God's best gift.")

I bet that you do what every member of our family does on Christmas Eve or Christmas Day—you open presents! (*Allow comments.*) If I can tell what might be a special gift, I save it until last. (*Show them the two presents*).

If both of these gifts were for me, I would open this one first and save this nice one for last. (*Open them, finding something tattered and old in the first, and something nice, perhaps a new coloring book, in the second.*) We like to save the best until last.

In our story Jesus was invited to a wedding, and the host served the best wine first. He thought that near the end of the party he could bring out the least expensive wine, and the guests wouldn't notice or wouldn't care. But that is not the way God gave his best gift to the world.

God saved his best gift, his Son, until just the right time. God had sent other people as gifts, and we read about them in the Bible. Some were prophets or judges. Some, like Moses, were great leaders. Those people did all they could do to show others the way to God. But the people still did not realize how much God loved them.

So on Christmas Day God gave to the world his best gift. Do you know who was born at Christmas in a manger in Bethlehem? (*Jesus.*) Yes, Jesus was God's best gift ever. Jesus taught great truths, healed the sick, and fought against evil. He was killed on a cross and raised from the dead and we can pray to him every day. In everything Jesus said or did, he showed the people around him—and you and me—that God truly loves us. God loves us so much that he gave us the best gift he could give—Jesus our Savior.

—R.J.C.

Third Sunday in Epiphany

The Gospel: Luke 4:14-21

Focus: Jesus dared to read from Scripture and say it was about himself.

Experience: The children will see that Jesus was someone who knew he was called by God.

A Very Nervy Person

Some Sundays when I come back into the sanctuary after the worship service is over, I find someone standing at the lectern where the Bible is read (*point to the lectern*) or at the pulpit where the good news is preached (*point to the pulpit*). If the microphone is on, that person has a good time making his or her voice sound big, playing the part of the minister.

In Luke chapter 4 we read that Jesus did something like that. All the people of Nazareth had come to worship God in the synagogue. Jesus stood up, went to the lectern where the Scriptures were read, and read from the book of Isaiah. When he finished, he went back to his seat, and then something different happened. Jesus stood up again and began to preach. He said the Bible passage he had read was about *him*.

Well, he had some nerve, don't you think? Jesus said he was the one God had promised to send. He was the one who would preach good news to the poor and set things right for those who had been wronged.

Would any of you have the courage to get up in church and talk to everyone like that? (*Allow responses.*) I know I wouldn't. Would one of you dare to go up to the lectern and read from the Bible and then go back to your seat and stand up again and begin to preach that God had picked you to save the world? No, we wouldn't. But Jesus knew he was special.

Jesus wasn't playing a game, and he wasn't just fooling around. He knew that what he said might lead to trouble, but he knew God had sent him to do special work for God. And he was ready to tell the people about it. What good things did Jesus do? How did he help sick people? hungry people? (*Allow responses.*) Finally he was killed on the cross and raised from the dead. Jesus *was* special. He is the Savior of the world.

(*This sermon anticipates the continuation of the story from Luke 4 for next Sunday. You may choose to suggest the story will be continued next Sunday.*)   **—R.J.C.**

Fourth Sunday in Epiphany
————————————— • —————————————

The Gospel: Luke 4:21-32

Focus: Jesus became unpopular when his audience realized he meant for the kingdom (church) to include every kind of person.

Experience: The children will realize that our own church is not complete unless it includes many different kinds of people, especially those we think don't fit or don't belong.

When Is Our Church Complete?

(Hold the lectern Bible in front of the children and with reverence open it to Luke 4. While tracing around the outer edge with your index finger, say, "This is the Word of God and today we hear the rest of the story about Jesus returning to Nazareth.")

Last Sunday we heard about Jesus reading from Scripture and then speaking as someone who knew what those words meant. He said God had sent him to do special work. At first the people were pleased with what he said.

But as we read on, just a few lines more, these same people became very angry at Jesus. They threw him out of their synagogue, they threw him out of their town, and they were ready to throw him over a cliff, hoping he would be killed. Do you wonder what Jesus said or did that caused them to become so angry?

One thing Jesus seemed to be saying was this: Our church isn't complete. There are other kinds of people who should be here. What would you think if Jesus came to our church and said to us, "Your church isn't complete. There are other kinds of people who should be here"? Let's talk about who those people might be. What kind of people don't you like? *(Allow responses and offer hints if needed: someone who was mean to you, someone who picked a fight with you, bad people, robbers, etc.)* Jesus said the church needs to include people who aren't wanted and who aren't liked, people who may have spent time in prison and people like those you see on television or on the streets of *(name of closest city)* who wear old and smelly clothes. God loves them all.

What do you think? Would we be angry with Jesus if he told us that our church needed a lot of different people, people we think

don't belong here? Maybe we would. But Jesus was trying to tell us
that God loves all people, and he wants us to love them, too.

                                                              —R.J.C.

Fifth Sunday in Epiphany
———————————————— • ————————————————

The Gospel: Luke 5:1-11

Focus: Jesus was some special kind of person.

Experience: The children will connect the experience of packing and leaving home with the experience of Peter, James, and John leaving everything in order to follow Jesus.

Preparation: Bring one or two suitcases.

Jesus Calls His First Disciples

(*Hold the lectern Bible in front of the children and with reverence open it to Luke 5. While tracing around the outer edge with your index finger, say,* "This is the Word of God and today we hear how Jesus called his first disciples.")

Our story from Luke says that Peter, James, and John left everything and followed Jesus. They became his disciples. It makes us think about Jesus. Jesus must have been some special kind of person for Peter, James, and John to leave home.

Who can remember the first time you spent a night away from home? (*Encourage the children to answer.*) Can you remember packing a suitcase and saying good-bye to Mom and Dad? Who can remember packing for camp when you would be gone for a week or longer? Or maybe you remember when your brother or sister did. What was it like being away from home? Did you get homesick? What did you miss the most? (*Allow responses.*) Your toys, your own bed, your pets, favorite foods, your parents, your brothers and sisters? And what if you were going to be gone for a long time? Would you miss your friends, your school if you go to school, your church, your parents? I can see you leaving now. You have suitcases in both hands. (*Place suitcases in front of you.*) You are saying good-bye. You're going on a trip, and you aren't sure where you are going to sleep the next night or what you will eat. Everything will be strange, and you will miss your home.

Luke says Peter, James, and John left everything behind—their home, their parents, even what they liked to do best of all, fishing in the Sea of Galilee. Jesus was some special kind of person.

"Come with me," he said, "and together we will build a kingdom of love and justice."

You don't have to leave home to help Jesus build his kingdom of love and justice. But if you begin to love Jesus as Peter, James, and John did, you never know what adventures you might have ahead of you! **—R.J.C.**

Sixth Sunday in Epiphany
————————————————•————————————————

The Gospel: Luke 6:17-26

Focus: Jesus the healer loved and accepted those who were sick.

Experience: The children will hug a teddy bear and connect the feeling of giving the teddy bear a hug with Jesus' love for the unlovely.

Preparation: Bring a teddy bear, preferably a little worn looking.

Jesus Loves Me, No Matter What

Everyone knows that a teddy bear likes to be hugged. (*Hug your teddy bear and let the children hug it too.*) Perhaps you never thought of it before, but Jesus liked to be hugged and to hug others. Luke says that all kinds of sick people "sought to touch him." In fact, I believe they may have pushed and shoved and pressed in until they were close enough for Jesus to touch them—or let us say, until they got a tender, loving, bear hug.

These were sick people. They were people with diseases and people that others did not want to touch because they were afraid to hug or to be hugged by them.

Let's pretend your teddy bear has gone through a lot. She is dirty. Her clothes are torn. Her ear is ragged. And she is sick besides. No other children would want your teddy bear, and they wouldn't think of giving her a hug! Not for a moment. But you are different. You know your teddy bear; they don't. You have loved your teddy bear through good times and bad times. It doesn't matter how she looks. You are going to hug her anyway.

And you are doing just what Jesus did. He knew what it was like to be sick and to be unloved. He hugged the sick and lonely people anyway, even when no one else would. And that was enough, as we learn from Luke, to make them well and whole again. —**R.J.C.**

Seventh Sunday in Epiphany

——————————— • ———————————

The Gospel: Luke 6:27-38

Focus: Jesus stopped the cycle of revenge by returning love for violence.

Experience: The children will talk about revenge, watch you refuse to hit back, and experience love as a different way to live in this world.

Love Is a Better Way

(*Hold the lectern Bible in front of the children and with reverence open it to Luke 6. While tracing around the outer edge with your index finger, say,* "This is the Word of God, and today we hear how Jesus did not get even.")

Does anyone here know what revenge is? (*Accept their answers and summarize.*) It is getting back or getting even. You hit me, so I hit you. You hit me harder, so I hit you harder still. You take what is mine, so I take what is yours. Revenge is what often happens on the playground at school, at home, and throughout the entire world. Nations try to get even with other nations, and people who live in the same nation try to take revenge on people of a different race. Don't you wish revenge could end? If only there was a way! (*Pause and let the children think about what you have said thus far.*)

What would happen if you hit me and I don't hit you back? What if you hit me and I *choose* not to get angry at you? What if I *choose* not to get revenge? What would happen if you stole something from me and I ask you if there is anything else I have that you need?

Wow! That would be different. That would be awesome.

I would like to try a little demonstration, and I will need one person to help me. (*To be realistic you need to lower yourself so that you are the same height.*) I want you to hit me on the arm. Pretend you are mad at me. You're in a bad mood. You're angry. (*Encourage the child to hit you. Then afterward say something like the following.*) I don't like it when you hit me (*rub your arm*), but I'm *not* going to hit you back. I'm not going to run away frightened either. Instead I'm going to tell you that I care about you. I would care if you got sick, and I would care if you got hurt. I care if you are happy, and I care if you are sad.

Do you feel like hitting me again? You probably would if I hit you back. And the hitting would continue back and forth. But we can act in a different way. We can act the way Jesus acted. Even when he was nailed to a cross, he loved those who wanted to harm him because he knew *love* was a better way than revenge. (*You may want to hug each other as a way to show love.*)   **—R.J.C.**

Eighth Sunday in Epiphany
—————————————————— • ——————————————————

The Gospel: Luke 6:39-49

Focus: Forgiveness comes more easily when we recognize that we are not perfect, that we are in need of forgiveness.

Experience: The children will observe a demonstration of how we make fun of others although we offend as much as they do.

Preparation: Make or find two silly hats. Arrange in advance with another adult to wear one of the hats and to make fun of you and the hat you are wearing.

I Can't See What's Wrong With Me

(*Hold the lectern Bible in front of the children and with reverence open it to Luke 6. While tracing around the outer edge with your index finger, say,* "This is the Word of God, and today we hear about forgiveness.")

(*You wear one of the hats. Begin by saying to the other adult:*) "I've seen it all. How can you come to church wearing a silly hat? Well, I just can't imagine someone being so silly. I mean, like, wake up and smell the coffee. Like, get a life, would you please."

(*Your partner says:*) "Are you speaking to me? Look what's on top of your head! Can't you see the silly hat *you're* wearing? I mean, like, why don't *you* get a life?"

(*You reply:*) "Who, me?" (*Feel the hat and then roll your eyes upward.*) "Why, I *am* wearing a silly hat. I guess . . . I guess I was too busy making fun of you and your hat to notice it." (*Partner leaves.*)

I would like you to think about this. Everyone here does some things wrong, maybe even wearing silly hats. We are not perfect. We make mistakes. We hurt other people. We make fun of others. What are some ways you have made mistakes? (*Allow responses*). We can forgive others because *we* need to be forgiven, too, and God is willing to forgive all of us.

I would like you to pray with me about this. (*Slowly make the transition to prayer by taking off your hat so there is time for the children to process what they have witnessed.*)

"Dear God, it is true that there are times when I can easily see what is wrong with someone else and make fun of them. Help me, dear God, to see that I am not perfect and that I also might be wearing a silly hat and hurting other people by what I say. Together, let us forgive one another. Amen."   —R.J.C.

The Transfiguration of Our Lord— Last Sunday in Epiphany

————————————————— • —————————————————

The Gospel: Luke 9:28-36

Focus: There are special experiences when we momentarily see Jesus in his full glory—as the Son of God.

Experience: The children will see how light can be even brighter when conditions are different.

Preparation: A flashlight and a heavy blanket.

Seeing Jesus in a Different Light

(*Hold the lectern Bible in front of the children and with reverence open it to Luke 9. While tracing around the outer edge with your index finger, say,* "This is the Word of God, and today we see how Jesus was recognized as the Son of God.")

This morning we will try to understand how Jesus was the Son of God. It will not be easy. But let's give it a try.

When I turn on this flashlight, you can barely see it because this room is so full of light. (*Flash the light around.*) But if we get under this heavy blanket and turn on this flashlight, the very same light looks very bright. (*As many as possible crawl under the blanket with you. Then crawl out.*) Wasn't the flashlight bright when we were in the dark? (*Yes.*)

Jesus had a lot of friends, but his very special friends were called disciples. When they walked and talked with Jesus and when they saw the wonderful ways he taught and healed, they knew that he was a very special person. But they thought Jesus was still just a human person like themselves. He was a bright light in the bright light of day, so they did not see anything more than a wonderful man.

Then one day Jesus and his disciples went up on a mountain, and the disciples saw something they had never seen before. They saw a special light around Jesus, shining so brightly that they understood that Jesus was also the Son of God. (*Shield your eyes as if seeing a bright light.*) That brightness did not last very long, however. It quickly faded, and everything returned to the way it was.

And yet those disciples began to understand that Jesus was very special.

Remember how the flashlight seemed brighter under the blanket? On that mountaintop for a moment Jesus shone brighter, and the disciples knew he was special.

"Dear God, we give thanks that Jesus is our friend. We also give thanks for those moments when we see Jesus shine so brightly that we know that he is the Son of God. Amen."   **—R.J.C.**

First Sunday in Lent

————————————•————————————

The Gospel: Luke 4:1-13

Focus: Jesus was able to resist temptation. Children can also resist temptation with God's help.

Experience: Through a story about children like them, the children will experience the often quiet, yet strong voice of temptation.

Preparation: Practice telling the story below. Find or draw a picture of an ice-cream truck with a bell on it. The bell should have a face. Other props for the story are optional. (A billfold is mentioned.)

Sometimes We Are Tempted

Good morning, children. It is good to see you this morning. Is anyone here for the first time? (*If so, introduce yourself and welcome the child or children*).

First, I would like to know from each of you what your favorite ice cream flavor is. (*Have the children answer.*) OK, I need your help with something. But first, listen to this story.

Once or twice a week, usually in the afternoon, a small truck drives down our street. It's white and has red balloons painted on it. It plays children's music through a loudspeaker and rings a bell every so often. Do you know what kind of truck that is? (*Allow time for responses. The children will probably guess it.*) Right, it's the ice-cream truck. (*Hold up a picture of one.*)

The other day, the ice-cream truck again came through our neighborhood, playing music and ringing the bell. A lot of children, children like yourselves, went up to the truck to buy ice cream. Two children in my neighborhood, Charley and Chris, wanted ice cream, too, but they did not have any money. They had already spent their money at the mall and at the store. But they wanted ice cream so much—especially Charley. So they looked for some money everywhere in their house—under the sofa, in the cracks of the big armchair, in the pockets of all their pants and coats. They even shook their piggy banks to see if any money would come out.

The ice-cream truck came closer and closer to their house. They could hear the music from the loudspeakers and the ringing of the bell. The bell seemed to be talking to them: "Come, quickly. Buy some ice cream!" it seemed to say. "Come, quickly!"

Chris and Charley really wanted to get some ice cream, but they could not find any money—not in their bedrooms, not in the living room, not in the den. Then they got to the kitchen. And on the counter they saw mom's grocery list and her billfold, full of coins and bills. (*Place a billfold in front of the children.*) They stopped and looked at each other.

"Come quickly. Get some ice cream," the bell seemed to say. "But we don't have any money," they thought. They looked at each other, at the billfold, and then out the window at the ice-cream truck coming slowly up the street. "But there is money in the billfold on the counter," the bell seemed to say. "Take it, quickly, and come and buy some ice cream." The children made a step toward the billfold. Charley stretched out one arm, ready to grasp it. (*Have the children stretch out their arms along with you.*) The bell kept calling to them: "Go ahead. No one will notice. You can always lie about it later. Come, get some ice cream, quickly." (*Stop the story here.*)

This is where I need your help. The Gospel lesson today tells about the devil asking Jesus to do things that were wrong in the eyes of God. If we think of that story, what should Charley and Chris do? Listen to the voice of the bell, steal the money, buy the ice cream, and lie about it later if asked about it? (*Allow time for responses, affirm answers about resisting temptation. Help those who said they would steal the money to think of better ways to get ice cream or things they like. Tell them God will help us say no to temptations.*) Would that be right in the eyes of God? (*Again, affirm answers about resisting the temptation.*) Would God say it is OK to steal money and to lie about it? (*No.*) Should we listen to God or listen to others—like the voice of the bell on the ice-cream truck? We should do what God wants, and we can pray for God to help us say no to temptation. The story of Jesus and the devil teaches us that we should listen first of all to God, especially when other voices are trying to get us to do things that God does not like. And the best place to hear what God wants for us is in Sunday school and in worship service. I am glad you are here today!   **—N.F.H.**

Second Sunday in Lent

————————————•————————————

The Gospel: Luke 13:31-35

Focus: Jesus healed people, and God provides healing for us in many ways.

Experience: The children will be asked to remember pain, illness, or injury that they have experienced and then to relate them to the many ways God provides healing for us.

Preparation: Bring a piece of medical equipment such as a brace, a crutch, aspirin, a bandage.

God Can Help Us

Good morning, children. Is anyone here for the first time? (*If so, introduce yourself and welcome the child or children.*)

What is this? (*Point to the piece of medical equipment you have brought and listen to responses.*) What is it used for? (*To help us walk, get well, or to get along better.*) Who uses it? (*Let the children answer.*)

Have any of you ever been hurt so that you had to wear a brace or a bandage or use crutches or take medicine? Tell me what happened. (*Allow time for responses. If the children do not describe many different hurts, ask them to mention what parts of the body could get hurt and how they could be fixed. You may want to write the responses down. You will need them later.*)

In the Gospel lesson for today Jesus says, "Listen, I am casting out demons and performing cures." That is another way of saying, "Listen, I am making people well again. I am taking care of their hurts and pains and illness." The Bible contains many stories about Jesus healing and curing sick people or those who were not able to see or to walk.

You mentioned quite a few kinds of hurts and sicknesses. How about us today? Does God help us get well? What kind of *people* help us when we get hurt or sick? (*The children will probably say Mom and Dad, friends, teachers, doctors, nurses.*) God gives us those people to help us and comfort us. If we are *really* sick or need an operation, where might we need to go for a while? (*Hospital.*) And we might have to take medicine or wear bandages or have a shot or use crutches for a while—all of those things help us get better, and they are gifts from God, too. All the time God is helping our bodies get better, helping them heal in answer to our prayers.

Let's name some of the sicknesses, hurts, and pains that we mentioned before. After I say each one, I will ask you, "Can God help us when we have _____ (blank)?" Then you answer, "God helps us get well!" (*Use several illnesses and injuries: Can God help us when we have the flu, a skinned knee, a headache, etc.? Assist the children as needed in their response of "God helps us get well!"*) Thank you! Now everyone here today has heard what you said. God helps us in many ways when we are sick or hurting—through family and friends, through doctors and nurses, or directly. Let's all say it together: "Thank you, God, for helping us get well." (*Children say it with you.*)   —N.F.H.

Third Sunday in Lent

————————————— • —————————————

The Gospel: Luke 13:1-9

Focus: As Christians grow in their faith lives, they are expected to "bear good fruit," that is, to become more loving, joyful, peaceful, patient, kind, generous, faithful, gentle, and self-controlled (Gal. 5:22-23).

Experience: In analogy to the Gospel story, the children will be asked to role-play trees that grow and bear fruit and trees that fail to bear fruit but which are given a second chance.

Preparation: Bring either real fruit (apples) or pictures (may be hand-drawn) of individual fruits. You need at least one piece or picture of fruit for each child. Keep them in a bag so that they remain hidden from sight until needed. Ask two confident children to play the parts of trees that do not bear fruit.

A Second Chance

Good morning, children. I am very glad to see you here. Is anyone here for the first time? (*If so, introduce yourself and welcome the child or children.*)

Today I have a riddle for you. Listen and see if you can figure out what I am talking about. If you think you know the answer, raise your hand, but don't say anything so that everyone has a chance to think about it.

Here we go: It is red but sometimes green and sometimes yellow and red. It starts out small but gets bigger as it gets older. It hangs up high while it grows, but when it is all grown up it comes down to the ground. What is it? (*Allow time for thought, elicit several answers before affirming or revealing the correct one.*) Right. I am talking about an apple, like this one here. (*Pull one out of the bag.*) I love apples. They are my favorite fruit. What are your favorite fruits? (*Give each child a chance to reply.*)

We all know that you can *buy* fruit like apples and (*name fruits mentioned by the children*) in the store. But where do apples and _____ and _____ come from? (*Insert fruits mentioned by children, avoiding fruit that does not grow on trees.*) Right. They grow on trees. So, what do you call a tree if bananas grow on it? Right, a banana tree. What do you call a tree with cherries? A cherry tree. (*You may also name others.*)

Now I want all of you to pretend to be trees. And I am going to pretend to be the farmer who owns the trees. First, you are very, very small. So, get down and be small. Then year after year you get a little older and bigger. (*Have the children slowly straighten up and spread their arms as branches*). Then, one day you are big enough to bear fruit. And apples or oranges or cherries will grow on you. (*Place paper fruits or real fruit in children's hands, except the two to whom you talked ahead of time about their roles. Have them fold their arms.*)

Hey, what is going on here? You are supposed to grow fruit like the other trees. I want you to grow fruit. If you don't do that, I'll have to remove you. Well, maybe you are just having a bad year. I will wait until next summer. I will pick the other fruit and wait till next year. (*Pick the fruit off the children's hands.*)

Then fall came and the trees lost their leaves. (*Have children lower their arms.*) And they were cold during the winter. (*Shiver.*) But spring came again and summer, and the trees grew some more. (*Stand on toes.*) And they bore fruit. (*Put fruits into children's hands.*) Now how about those two trees that didn't have any fruit last year? (*Ask the two how they are doing. They will probably want to bear fruit. Give them some.*) Now look at all the trees. Every one has fruit!

Do you know why the farmer gave those two trees another chance to bear some fruit? He acted that way because that is how things are in today's Gospel lesson. We heard about a fig tree that did not grow any figs for three years. They said it could have one more year to produce fruit. So we gave our trees one more year, too! We gave them another chance.

God is like that. Even if we do things wrong, God often gives us another chance. We are thankful for God's patience. And because we get another chance, we are more likely to do what God wants us to do, such as being kind and loving, patient and gentle, peaceful and joyful.

Thank you, children, for being such good trees! (*Collect paper fruits, but if real fruit was used, let each child keep one.*)   **—N.F.H.**

Fourth Sunday in Lent

—————————————— • ——————————————

The Gospel: Luke 15:1-3, 11-32

Focus: The story of the prodigal son teaches us about God's patience and love.

Experience: The children will provide pantomime related to the actions and emotions of the characters in the Gospel.

Preparation: Practice the pantomime that goes with the story. You may wish to recruit an adult to read the story, pausing at the appropriate moments, so that you can concentrate on modeling the pantomine. If time is short, you could stop with the return of the younger son, the last line being, "And they began to celebrate."

The Younger Son Changes His Mind

Good morning, children. It is good to see you here. Is anyone here for the first time? (*If so, introduce yourself and welcome the child or children.*)

Today I am going to ask you to help me act out a story. There are no speaking parts but lots of gestures. _____ (*insert name*) will read the story to us, and I will teach you a number of motions as we go along. So pay close attention to the story, and do what I am doing. Let's all stand up. You do the motions that I do.

Jesus told this story:

There was a man who had two sons. The younger of them said to his father, "Father, give me the money that will belong to me." (*Stretch out your right hand as if receiving something, wave with your left hand to indicate that something should be given to you and faster.*) So the father divided his property between his two sons. (*With your right hand take imaginary stuff out of your left hand and give it to two imaginary persons.*)

A few days later the younger son gathered all that he had and traveled to a far-away place. (*Walk in place.*) There he spent all his money on sports and gambling and eating and drinking. (*Pretend to be giving something away with your hands. Pretend to pay with money.*)

When he had spent all his money (*pretend to be looking for money in pockets, stretch out your hands, look disappointed, shrug your shoul-*

ders) he wasn't able to buy any more food. (*Hold your stomach as if in hunger pain, make pain-filled face, stretch out cupped hands as if begging.*)
So he went and worked for a man who sent him to feed pigs. (*Pretend to be throwing food to the pigs from a bucket in your other hand then sit down.*) He would gladly have eaten the pigs' food (*lick your lips and smack your lips*), but no one gave him anything. (*Throw up your hands and shrug your shoulders.*)

Then it finally dawned on him (*hit your forehead softly with your right hand*) that his father's servants had plenty to eat. He decided to go to his father and say to him, "Father, I have sinned against heaven and before you. I am no longer worthy to be called your son. Treat me like one of your servants." So he got up and went to his father. (*Get up and walk in place.*)

But while he was quite a long way from home, his father saw him. (*Place your hand against your forehead as if shielding your eyes from the sun while looking for someone. Show happy surprise on your face.*) The father was filled with love, and he ran (*run in place*) and put his arms around him (*pretend to be hugging someone*) and kissed him (*pretend to be kissing someone*).Then the son said to the father (*fold your hands as if sorry, bow your head, and look to the ground*). "Father, I have sinned against heaven and before you. I am no longer worthy to be called your son." But the father said to his servants, "Quickly, bring out a robe (*make the waving hand motion that indicates "bring it here"*)—the best one—and put it on him (*pretend to be putting a robe on someone*), put a ring on his finger (*pretend to do so*) and sandals on his feet (*pretend to put sandals on your feet*). Get the fatted calf and kill it, and let us eat and celebrate. This son of mine was dead and is alive again. He was lost and is found." And they began to celebrate. (*Clap your hands, dance around, smile.*)

Now the other son was in the field, and when he came to the house (*walk in place*), he heard music and dancing (*put your hand to your ear as if listening to something*). He called one of the servants (*use your index finger for a "come here" signal*) and asked what was going on. The servant replied, "Your brother has come home, and your father has killed the fatted calf because he got him back safe and sound." Then the older brother became angry and refused to go in to the party. (*Fold your arms in defiance, make a pouting or angry face.*)

His father came out and pleaded with him. (*Join your hands in pleading or begging position in front of your chest.*) But he answered his father, "Listen! (*Shake your index finger as if admonishing someone.*) For all these years I have been working like a slave for you, and I have never disobeyed your command. Yet you have never let me have a party. But when this son of yours who has wasted half of your money, comes back, you throw this big party and invite everyone!"

Then the father said to him, "Son, you are always with me (*pretend to hug someone*), and all that is mine is yours. But we had to celebrate and rejoice because I thought this brother of yours was probably dead, and now I know he is alive. He was lost and has been found."   **—N.F.H.**

Fifth Sunday in Lent

———————————— • ————————————

The Gospel: Luke 20:9-19

Focus: Christians share freely what they have because they have received freely from others and from God.

Experience: The children will receive something freely from the pastor or leader who had received it freely. Then the children will share freely with the congregation.

Preparation: Bring a whole bunch of an item that can be easily shared (cookies, candies, carrot sticks, grapes, peanuts in shells, pennies, gum, etc.). Keep them hidden from the children (in a bag or container) until you are ready to use them in the sermon. You will also need a note saying: "Dear _____ (*insert your name*), Yesterday I received a whole bunch of these. It was a big surprise, and I was very happy. I wanted to share my surprise gift and my joy with you." (*The handwriting on the note should not be your handwriting.*)

Sharing Freely

Good morning, children, I am very happy to see all of you here today. Is anyone here for the first time? (*If so, introduce yourself and welcome the child or children.*)

Yesterday, after I woke up, I wanted to go out of the house to get my newspaper. I opened the kitchen door easily, but the storm door, which opens to the outside, seemed stuck. Actually, a box (basket, jar, bucket, bowl, plate) full of _____ (*insert name of items that you brought*) was sitting in front of the storm door. So I had to push to get the door open. Why would anyone put a box (*or whatever*) full of _____ (*name it*) in front of my door? However, there was a little note attached to it. (*Show it to children.*) My neighbor had written it to me. It said: Dear _____ (*insert your name*), Yesterday I received a whole bunch of these. It was a big surprise, and I was very happy. I wanted to share my surprise gift and my joy with you."

I was curious. After I got dressed, I went over to my neighbor's house to find out more about this mysterious gift. "It came from my aunt," my neighbor said. "She left four boxes (*or whatever*) of these in front of my door yesterday."

"Where did she get that many?" I asked.

"From her neighbor, and he got twice as much."

"And where did your aunt's neighbor get all of them?" I still wanted to know where they came from.

"He got them from a friend who says he got them from God."

"From God?" I asked.

"Yes," my neighbor said, "the friend is a farmer, and he believes that everything in the world is a gift from God to make us happy and to show us how much he loves us. So the farmer just wanted to pass on the happiness and love. So did his friend and my aunt, and so did I."

Well, children, here is my box (*or whatever*) full of _____ . Considering what all the other people did, and why, what should I do? (*Elicit answers. Affirm any about generosity or sharing God's gifts.*) Right, and I will share with you. Well, here you go. (*Distribute what you brought evenly to all children. Make sure each child gets more than one.*) Here is my last question. Now that I have shared my surprise gift and my happiness with you, how do you feel? (*Responses.*) Happy and surprised, I hope. And what is the next thing that you are going to do? Right, share with someone else. As a matter of fact, let us do that right now. Get up and go out into the congregation and share your _____ (*name it*) with someone else. Thanks.   —N.F.H.

Sunday of the Passion—Palm Sunday

————————————•————————————

The Gospel: Luke 22:1—23:56

Focus: Jesus died so that we might live.

Experience: The children will learn to say "Jesus Died for Me," using sign language.

Preparation: Practice the four words in sign language so that you can comfortably teach them.

Jesus Died So That We Might Live

Good morning, children. It is good to have you all here today. Is anyone here for the first time? (*If so, introduce yourself and welcome the child or children.*)

Today we started our worship a bit differently from other Sundays. What did we do differently? (*Await responses. Adapt the following to fit your situation.*) Right, we gathered outside, everyone got a palm branch, we said a prayer, I read from the Bible, then we all entered the building singing a hymn. We did this because today is a special Sunday. Does anyone know the name of this Sunday? (*Await responses.*) Right, this Sunday is called Passion Sunday or Palm Sunday because in our Gospel lesson today we hear how people threw palm branches onto the road when Jesus entered the city of Jerusalem. We also heard how Jesus was arrested and taken to court and then crucified. The story is quite long and quite sad. If Jesus was so good and loved everyone, why did he have to die?

The Bible tells us that there was a plan. Jesus had done nothing wrong, but everybody else who has ever lived—and that includes you and me—has done things wrong—both little things and big things. Jesus took the punishment for all those wrong things on himself. Jesus died for us. Then he rose again on Easter. He is alive! We are very thankful for all that Jesus has done for us.

Today I am going to teach you how to say "Jesus died for me" in sign language. Does anyone know what sign language is? (*Allow responses.*) Yes, it's speaking with our hands. Some people have trouble hearing, and some can't hear at all. Sign language helps them because they can talk with their hands. We can learn sign language, too.

Jesus

This is the sign for *Jesus*. (*Demonstrate the sign.*) Now you try it. (*All do it together. Repeat it several times.*)

died   for   me.

This is the sign for *died*. (*Demonstrate each sign and repeat the previous process for the remaining words.*) This is the sign for *for*. This is the sign for *me*.

Now let's see if we can do all four words so that we can give the message, *Jesus died for me*. (*Do them, repeating if necessary.*) Let's face the congregation and do the four signs. This time we will use our voices and say, "Jesus died for me" as we sign. (*Do this.*) Thank you. I hope you will remember these four words. They tell us that Jesus is our Savior, that Jesus is our friend. **—N.F.H.**

The Resurrection of Our Lord—Easter Day

—————————————— • ——————————————

The Gospel: John 20:1-9 (10-18)

Focus: When Mary was called by her name, she recognized Jesus. Being called by our names catches our attention, and we become aware of the person who is calling us.

Experience: The children will talk about their names and the importance of names. They will be reassured that Jesus is alive and that he loves them.

Called by Name

I'm so glad you are here today. Today has a special name. Do you know what name we have for this day? (*Easter.*) Very good.

Names are very important, so let's look at some other names. Who has a cat or dog or other pet? (*Responses.*) What are their names? (*Responses.*) Now suppose I came to your house (*pick one child*) and I called your (*cat, dog*) _____ (*use a different name than the child said*). Would you think I knew your (*cat, dog*) very well? (*No.*)

What about your brothers and sisters? Who has a brother or sister? (*Responses.*) What are their names? (*Field several.*) What if you called your brother or sister _____ (*use a different name, maybe an animal's name.*) What would he or she think? (*Responses.*)

How about you? When someone calls you by your name, what do you do? (*Look, come, listen, etc.*) Of course you do. Do you think people know you if they use your name? (*Yes.*)

Something like this happened to Mary Magdalene that first Easter morning when she went to the cave where Jesus' body had been taken after he died on the cross. When she got there, the cave was empty. Jesus was not there. She started crying because she thought someone had stolen Jesus' body. Then someone started talking to her, but she didn't know who it was. Do you remember who it was? (*Jesus.*)

It was Jesus. What did Jesus do so that Mary would know who he was? (*Responses.*) He called her by name. He said, "Mary." Then she knew it was Jesus. Jesus had risen. He was alive. Jesus knew her name, and Jesus knows each of your names, too. Jesus loves each one of you. **—M.C.A. and G.W.**

Second Sunday of Easter

————————————•————————————

The Gospel: John 20:19-31

Focus: As one of Jesus' close friends and followers, Thomas did not want to be left out. He wanted to see Jesus, and Jesus came to him.

Experience: The children will see how it feels to be left out.

Preparation: Bring a bag or box with something interesting in it, perhaps a plant or flowers (symbols of new life appropriate for the Easter season). Arrange for someone to be the person who is left out, perhaps a youth or adult from the congregation.

Feeling Left Out

I'm glad you are here today! What do I have here? (*Hold up bag or box.*) Who thinks there is something inside it? (*Shake it. Wait for responses.*) Now how many of you think there is something inside it? (*Responses.*) What do you suppose it is? (*Field several responses, including comments that they need more clues.*) Does anyone want to see inside? (*Responses.*)

   OK, let's do this. I'm going to show this to everyone except one volunteer. Who wants to volunteer to be left out? (*If there is one, fine. Otherwise have someone else available.*) OK, you (*the volunteer*) stay over there. I'm going to show this to everyone else. (*To the group*) Can you keep a secret? Here we go. (*Show them the contents.*) Now, (*volunteer*), how do you feel? (*Prompt if necessary: left out, wishing I could see, etc.*) Do you want to see it? OK, here you go. (*Show it to the volunteer.*) (*You might also want to show the plant or whatever was in the bag to the congregation at this time.*)

   Nobody likes to be the only one left out. When Jesus came back to see the disciples after he rose from the dead on Easter, everybody had seen him except Thomas. Do you suppose Thomas wanted to see Jesus, too? (*Yes.*) Of course he did. Do you know if Thomas ever got to see Jesus again? (*Yes.*) You're right. Jesus wanted Thomas to know that he was alive, and he wants us to know too! Not one of us is left out. We all know that Jesus is alive!

—M.C.A. and G.W.

Third Sunday of Easter
—————————————— • ——————————————

The Gospel: John 21:1-14

Focus: We do not always recognize what we see until someone helps us. We do not always recognize God at work or Jesus' presence until someone helps us.

Experience: The children will look at an optical illusion.

Preparation: Bring an optical illusion to show the children, perhaps the vase-or-profiles illusion, or the old-hag-or-young-woman one.

What Do You See?

Today we're going to look at just how well we see things. Let me warn you that I just might try to trick you if I can! Let's get started by thinking about a street in our town (*or city or neighborhood*). Way down the street you saw something, but it was so far away that it looked like a black dot. Would you know what you saw? (*Probably not.*) Could it be a car? Could it be (*pause dramatically*) an elephant? Now we wouldn't expect to see an elephant in (*Oklahoma City, Clarkfield, etc.*), but that far away you wouldn't know for sure, would you? (*Responses.*)

That was very good, but let's try this. Have you ever looked for something and missed it even though it was right under your nose? (*Give an example, such as car keys. Allow responses.*)

So sometimes we don't see all we think we do, do we? Now look at this. (*Show optical illusion, the old-hag-or-young-woman or the vase-or-profiles.*) What do you see in this picture? (*Encourage both points of view.*) Who thinks it's a vase (or old woman)? (*Responses.*) Who thinks it's two faces looking at each other (or a young woman)? (*Responses.*) Could it be both? (*Responses.*)

You know that after Jesus rose from the dead on Easter, he came back to be with the disciples. But they didn't expect to see him, so they didn't recognize him at first. It was something like our examples. (*Mention dot at the end of the street or the optical illusion*).

But finally the disciples did recognize him. He came to the place where they were fishing and saw they weren't catching anything. So he told them what to do, and they caught lots of fish. Then the disciples knew it was Jesus, because he was able to do such marvelous things. They knew he was the Lord. We know Jesus is the Lord, too. We know who he is!   **—M.C.A. and G.W.**

Fourth Sunday of Easter

————————————— • —————————————

The Gospel: John 10:22-30

Focus: We often know what something is by what it does. We can know something about people by what they do. We know who Jesus is by what he did.

Experience: The children will see how an unusual object works.

Preparation: Bring an unusual object, perhaps a tool used for cooking, for woodworking, or for gardening; perhaps a musical instrument like a clarinet that has been taken apart but you can put back together. Put the object in a box or bag so the children won't see it until you show it to them.

We Know What Jesus Did

I'm glad you are in church with me today. Would any of you be surprised if I told you that Jesus is the Son of God? (*No.*) That was really too easy a question, wasn't it? (*Yes.*) Would any of you be surprised if I told you that when Jesus lived on earth, some people, even really smart ones, did not know he was the Son of God? (*Responses.*) Let's see how that could be.

Take a look at what I brought along. (*Take object out of box or bag.*) Does anyone know what this is or what you would use it for? (*Responses. Encourage them with appropriate questions. Would it work this way? What if I put these pieces together? Have you seen anyone use one of these? Finally say what it is, and tell what it does if they haven't figured it out.*) Very good. We solved the mystery because now we know what it does. We can know what something is by what it does.

Now let's go back to our question about why some people in Jesus' day, even though they were very smart, didn't know that he was the Son of God. The problem was that some people never got a chance to hear what he said or see what he did. Most of the people who watched Jesus heal people and saw his kindness and heard him teach *knew* he was the Son of God. But we live 2000 years later. We can't watch what Jesus did in his day. So how can we know that he is the Son of God? (*Responses. Help them if needed: the Bible tells us about what Jesus said and did, we learn about him in church, our teachers tell us, and we can pray to him.*) So we found out what this (*hold up object*) was by what it did. And we can know Jesus is the Son of God by what he did. He keeps on loving us every day!   **—M.C.A. and G.W.**

Fifth Sunday of Easter

———————————— • ————————————

The Gospel: John 13:31-35

Focus: We show that we are Jesus' disciples by loving others. We show that we are disciples by doing acts of service, both small and large.

Experience: The children will look at an item (or receive an item from you) and notice that they can see it and learn about it. Then they will think about whether they can see love or not.

Preparation: Bring an object that interests children, such as a music box or a ball. You may wish to bring something to distribute, such as M & M™ candies, pennies, or stickers.

What Does Love Look Like?

Today we are going to think about love. To help us, I've brought this. (*Show them the music box, ball, M & M™ candies, pennies, etc.*) Is this love? (*No.*) What is it? (*They give correct name.*) Right, this is (*give correct name*). Can you feel this? (*Let them do each action you mention.*) Can you smell this? Can you hear this? (*If unbreakable, drop it or thump it.*) Can you taste this (*for edible items*)? So we can find out what this (or these) look(s) like. And we can learn many other things about it (or them). (*If you brought something to give to the children, tell them that you will give them out at the end of the children's sermon.*)

Now what about love? Can you see love, or feel it, or hear it, or smell it, or taste it? (*Responses.*) We're not sure. Maybe we can; maybe we can't. We need to find out more. Do you think there really is such a thing as love? (*Yes.*)

Of course there is. When we do things that show love, love becomes real. And other people do things to show us that they love us, too. What are some of those things? (*Responses. Offer hints and examples. You or the children may mention some of the following: hugs and kisses; parents or others reading to them, giving them good food, clothes, presents; going places together; saying "I love you." Children can tell their parents they love them by doing chores, doing kind things for little brothers and sisters, doing other helpful actions.*)

The Bible tells us that Jesus told people that he loved them and that he wanted them to love one another. And do you know what? I think you know what love looks like. You know just what to do. (*If you brought candies or something to distribute, hand them out now.*)

—M.C.A. and G.W.

Sixth Sunday of Easter

————————————•————————————

The Gospel: John 14:23-29

Focus: Jesus assured his disciples that they would be able to remember him because the Holy Spirit would help them. He told them not to be troubled. He would give them peace.

Experience: The children will remember things they have been told and be reassured that they can remember Jesus and his love for them.

Remembering

Jesus told his disciples that he was going to heaven, but he did not want them to worry that they might forget him. He said that the Holy Spirit would help them to remember him.

Sometimes it is hard for us to remember things. Can you remember some things your mom or dad told you? What have they told you about themselves, especially about when they were children—what toys did they like? What kinds of things did they enjoy doing? Do you remember? (*Allow responses. Affirm them.*)

Sometimes we need to hear things over and over again to remember them. Sometimes we need to repeat things, like our address, so we will remember them. We might feel worried if we can't remember important things like 9-1-1 or another emergency telephone number.

The disciples wanted to remember all the good things about Jesus after he left them and went to heaven. We want to remember Jesus, too. Jesus tells us in the Bible, "Do not let your hearts be troubled, and do not let them be afraid." We don't have to be afraid that we will forget Jesus or that he will forget us.

Sometimes we are forgetful, but we know that we *can* remember Jesus and how much he loves us. Think of all the help we are getting. Who do we hear a lot about when we go to Sunday school? (*Jesus. They may name others, too, and that is fine.*) Who do we hear a lot about when we go to church and when someone reads the Bible to us and when we sing hymns? (*Jesus.*) Yes, so we *do* remember Jesus, and he tells us we don't need to be afraid because he will *always* love us. Now that is good news!   **—M.C.A. and G.W.**

Seventh Sunday of Easter
——————————————— • ———————————————

The Gospel: John 17:20-26

Focus: Jesus prayed for unity among all of his followers. Though there are many differences among us, we are all connected through God's love.

Experience: The children will notice differences and similarities between two people—you and one of the children.

Different or Alike?

Today we are going to look at some of the ways people are different and ways we are the same. Let's look at some differences first. I need a volunteer. (*If possible, choose a child of the gender opposite your own.*)

Thank you, (*name*). Now everybody, how are (*name*) and I different from each other? (*Listen to responses. As needed, add hints about height, gender, age, clothes, hair, where both live, food preferences, school attendance, pastimes, etc. Help to keep comments reasonably kind.*)

That was good. You found so many differences that I'm just about worn out! Now let's see how (*name*) and I are alike. (*Listen to responses. As needed, add hints about both being human beings; similar appearances such as hair, skin, or eye color; liking some of the same sports or foods; both attending church this morning; both are Christians.*)

Some of those last comments were right on target. And two important ways that *all* of us, not just (*name*) and me, are alike are these. Do we all love God? (*Yes*). And does God love all of us? (*Yes.*) You are right! So no matter what we look like, where we live, or what we eat, all of us are alike because God loves us. We are together in the love of God.   **—M.C.A. and G.W.**

The Day of Pentecost

———————————————————•———————————————————

The Gospel: John 15:26-27; 16:4b-11

Focus: On Pentecost we celebrate the birthday of the church.

Experience: The children will talk together about the church, its small beginnings, and how it grew. They will sing "Happy Birthday" to the church.

Preparation: Bring balloons or party hats for all the children. You might want to alert the organist to be ready to play the traditional "Happy Birthday" song at the end of the children's sermon.

It's the Church's Birthday!

Every year each of us celebrates the day we were born. In fact, we often have birthday parties, right? What do some of you do on your birthday? (*Allow a couple of responses. Try to keep them brief.*)

Do you know what birthday Christians are celebrating all over the world today? (*Responses. They probably won't know.*) It's the birthday of the church!

When you were born, you were quite little. About how long do you think you were? Let's measure with our hands. (*Hold your hands about twenty inches apart.*) Now look how tall you are!

How about the church? It started in one place with one group of people, but now think of all the churches we see. Where have you seen church buildings other than ours? (*Responses.*) Are there churches in other countries, too? (*Name some, especially any that ancestors of church members came from or places where missionaries you support live or places church members have visited.*) So the church, too, started out small and it grew and grew!

(*Distribute birthday items.*) So let's put on our birthday hats and hold our balloons high (*allow children to do so*), and let's all of us, adults and children, sing "Happy birthday, dear church." (*All join together, singing the traditional birthday song.*)   **—M.C.A. and G.W.**

The Holy Trinity—First Sunday after Pentecost

—————————————————•—————————————————

The Gospel: John 16:12-15

Focus: Children are filled with questions. Unanswered questions are as difficult for children as they are for adults. In our text Jesus decides which questions to answer and which to leave unanswered for the time being.

Experience: The children will listen to a story about a little girl who is filled with questions. Some of the questions can be answered immediately while others cannot.

Preparation: Practice telling the story. Avoid reading it. Draw a large question mark on a piece of tagboard.

But Why?

This morning I would like to tell you a story. It is about a little girl named Jennifer. Do we have any Jennifers here today? (*Responses.*) (*Show the large question mark on the tagboard, and ask the children if they know what it is. Tell the children that your story is about someone with lots of questions.*)

Once upon a time there was a little girl named Jennifer. Morning, noon, and night, she would ask her mother questions.

At the checkout lane in the grocery store Jennifer would ask how the cash register worked. While her mother drove down the street, Jennifer would ask her how the corner stoplight worked. One night at bedtime, Jennifer's mom was tucking her in. Jennifer folded her hands, closed her eyes, and prayed for her sister and her mother. When she opened her eyes again, she asked, "Why do I still see shapes and light when my eyes are closed?"

"I'll try to answer that question another time," her mom said. "But right now it's time to go to bed."

As Jennifer's mom pulled the blanket up, the little girl began to ask more questions. "Mom, may I have a glass of cold water from the bottle in the refrigerator?" Since it was a warm summer night, her mom agreed. When Mom returned with a cold glass of water, Jennifer immediately asked, "Mom, how does the refrigerator make the water cold?"

"Oh, Jennifer," her mom said, "I really can't explain that to you now."

"But, Mom, when you close the refrigerator door, does the light stay on?"

"That's all for now, Jennifer. Finish your drink and go to sleep." Every night was just the same. Jennifer would ask lots of questions and her mom would answer a few of them and put others off until later.

What do you have questions about? (*Responses.*) Where do you go to get answers? (*Responses.*)

In today's Bible story, Jesus' disciples had many questions for him. The questions were not about refrigerators but about what Jesus was going to do the next day and the day after that. Jesus said to them, "You have many questions. Don't worry. They will be answered when the time is right."

Jennifer had to trust that her mom would answer her questions sometime. The disciples had to trust Jesus, that Jesus would answer their questions sometime, too. The world is filled with lots of questions. We will find some of the answers but not others. Sometimes we don't know the answers to our questions, but we can trust Jesus whether we know the answers or not.   **—P.F.**

Second Sunday after Pentecost

————————————— • —————————————

The Gospel: Luke 7:1-10

Focus: As we hear about the healing of the centurion's slave, we are reminded again of God's grace and unconditional love.

Experience: The children will hear a story to remind them of what unconditional love is all about.

Preparation: If you choose to use the story as written, you might want to bring along a glove, bat, baseball cap or other objects that will help illustrate the story.

The Wrong Way, But That's OK

How many of you are happy today? How many are sad? Sometimes we may feel very happy and sometimes we may feel sad or worried. This morning our Bible story is about a man who was very sad and worried. He was sad because a man who worked for him, a man he liked very much was very sick and about to die. The first man heard that Jesus was coming by, so he sent some messengers to ask Jesus for help. As Jesus came closer, the man began to feel as though he wasn't important enough or good enough to ask Jesus for help. The man tried to send Jesus away, but Jesus kept coming. Finally the man said to Jesus, "Just say the word, and I know my servant will get better. And that's just what happened. Jesus said the man's servant would be healed, and at that moment he *was* healed. Jesus was impressed with the man's faith and love for his servant.

I have a friend named Andy who felt like the man in the story. He felt sad. One day when he was just a little older than some of you, Andy joined a baseball team. (*Show any baseball equipment you brought along.*) When he played in the outfield, he did a good job of *catching* the ball, but for some reason he just couldn't *hit* the ball.

The team had played six games, and Andy hadn't made one hit. He would try very hard, but he just couldn't hit the ball. The seventh game was to be played on Saturday, and it was a very special game for Andy. This was the first time his dad would be there to watch him play.

Andy came up to bat. The pitcher threw the ball. (*If you have room, you may want to swing the bat in pantomime as you mention each time Andy swung.*) Strike one! The pitcher threw the second ball. Strike two! Again the pitcher wound up and threw the ball. What do you think happened? (*Responses.*) Yes, this time he hit the ball! It went out between left field and center field.

Andy was so excited about hitting the ball that he began to run as fast as he could. But in his excitement he ran to third base instead of first base.

"Out!" The umpire called.

Andy felt so embarrassed! As he walked toward the bench, he wondered what the other kids would say. He wondered what the coach would do. He wondered what his dad thought. Walking slowly with his head hanging, he arrived at the bench.

The coach looked Andy in the eye and said, "Good hit, Andy, good hit."

When we don't think we are any good, when we mess up, when we fail to do what Mom or Dad asks, we too might feel like Andy. Have you ever felt like that? (*Responses.*) The Bible reminds us that Jesus is here to say, "I forgive you. Let's try again." No matter how bad you might feel, remember, Jesus is there to say, "I forgive you. I love you. Let's try again."   —P.F.

Third Sunday after Pentecost
———————————— • ————————————

The Gospel: Luke 7:11-17

Focus: Scripture contains many stories about the healing ministry of Jesus. This sermon will focus on what happened following
the healing of the son of the widow at Nain.

Experience: The children will talk about how news spreads in
our day and think about how the news of Jesus' healing of people
spread in his day and how they can spread the good news of Jesus'
love.

Preparation: Bring a front section of a daily newspaper with
some stories illustrating bad news and some stories reflecting good
news. You could also prepare a one-page handout that looks like
the front page of a newspaper or make a large front page on tagboard. The headline might read: Funeral Is Cancelled. The newspaper could be the *Nain Daily News.*
Your copy might go something like this:

> On _____ (select a date a few days ago) *in the city of Nain the
> fifteen-year-old son of a widow died of unknown causes. As they carried his
> body through the gate of the city on the way to the cemetery, a local teacher,
> known by some as Jesus as Nazareth, arrived near the gate. He was followed
> by disciples and others.*
>
> *Jesus of Nazareth noticed a large crowd of people with the grieving
> mother. It is reported that Jesus walked up to the mother and told her she
> would not have to cry any longer. He then went over to the boy, and said
> "Get up."*
>
> *To everyone's surprise the boy got up and began to speak. The news of this
> miracle spread very quickly as one person told another.*

Funeral Is Cancelled

This morning I brought a newspaper. On the front page there are
many sad stories. (*Mention a couple of the stories you find.*) Sometimes
we have to look back a few pages to find a story that is good news.
(*Mention a story or two that have good news in them.*) There is a story
about a cat that had been gone a long time but has found its way
home. Now that's good news, isn't it?

Our Bible story for today has some very good news in it. I wrote it like a newspaper story. Let me read it to you. (*Read from the one you have prepared.*)

As the news spread, more people began to talk about the love and compassion Jesus showed to those he met. One person would tell the next person and on and on until it seemed everyone knew the good news of the boy who came back to life.

Jesus also invites us to tell others about his love. The good news we have is that Jesus loves us and forgives us. Can you think of how we can tell others about Jesus' love? (*Wait for their answers.*)

Do you know that you have already told others the good news by just being here this morning? Look at all the people sitting in the church. You have reminded them of Jesus' love by being with us. You remind your friends in Sunday school when you are in class with them. You remind your family at home when you close your eyes, fold your hands, and pray at dinnertime.

In today's story Jesus is reminding us that we too need to tell others about him. (*Continue if you have a sheet to distribute.*) I have a front page for each of you. I have another front page for you to give to someone else. As you go back to your seat, would you please share the good news of Jesus' love? You can do that by giving this very special front-page story to someone you see on your way back to your seat. (*If you don't have the story to hand out, ask them when they return to their seats to tell someone that Jesus loves them. Say together, "Jesus loves you!"*)

Thanks for sharing the good news of Jesus with someone else!
—P.F.

Fourth Sunday after Pentecost
———————————— • ————————————

The Gospel: Luke 7:36-50

Focus: The Gospel lesson reminds us of Jesus' unconditional love, how he accepted a woman everyone else had rejected.

Experience: Through a story, open-ended questions, and the children's memories, they will be reminded of the kind of love Jesus offers.

Preparation: Practice telling the story. Avoid reading it. Personalize the story if possible. You will need drawings of two girls, one with a sad expression, the other with a happy expression. Find the words for the song, "Jesus Loves Me."

Jesus Loves Us

Once there were two sisters who were very different from each other. Jessica, the first sister, was very happy. (*Point to the picture of Jessica.*) When she woke up in the morning, she had a smile on her face. She would say, "Good morning, Mom" even before Mom could say hello to her. Jessica always tried to get along with her friends. When her younger sister's toys were scattered all over the living room, Jessica would even help pick them up.

Now Jessica's sister Madeline was very different. (*Point to the picture of Madeline.*) When she woke up in the morning, she was already angry. She would tease Jessica and try to pick a fight. She rarely smiled. She was not only unhappy, but she didn't think anyone liked her.

One day the girls' mom brought home a big box. Listening carefully, the girls could hear a scratching sound coming from inside. There were holes in the box, and they could hear something panting. Does anyone know what could have been in the box? (*Responses.*)

Quickly the girls opened the box, and there was a little puppy with dark, happy eyes, hair the color of caramel corn, and a tail that wouldn't stop wagging. Jessica was so happy she could not stop jumping up and down. Madeline sat there with a frown on her face and complained, "I don't like brown dogs."

As time went on, no matter what Madeline would do or say, the little puppy would try to get up into her lap and stand on his little back legs and lick Madeline's face. No matter how disinterested or unhappy Madeline looked, the puppy kept trying to be her friend. How have puppies or kittens treated you? (*Responses.*) Puppies seem to love *all* people, don't they?

That's the kind of love we have in our Bible lesson for today. It's a story about Jesus and a person like Madeline, a person who didn't think she could be loved, but Jesus loved her anyway. No matter what we do, even if we are like Madeline, Jesus keeps loving us.

I would like for us to sing about that kind of love. One of the first songs you ever learned in Bible school or Sunday school was a song that is still a favorite of mine. Can any of you guess what that song might be? (*Responses.*) "Jesus Loves Me." Let's sing it together. **—P.F.**

Fifth Sunday after Pentecost
————————————————— • —————————————————

The Gospel: Luke 9:18-24

Focus: Rumors regarding Jesus' identity were spreading. He wanted his disciples to believe that he was the Christ, the Messiah.

Experience: A name badge will be used in a conversation about Jesus' identity and the identity of the children.

Preparation: For each of the children you will need a stick-on name badge with a cross symbol on it. You may wish to have helpers ready with marker pens to write names on the badges before the children leave.

Who Are We?

This morning I am going to wear something special. (*Place a name badge on yourself.*) Do you like my name badge? On it I have written my name. There is also something else on the badge. What is it? (*Point to the cross. They will say, "A cross."*)

What does the cross tell you about me? (*If there are no good answers, respond by saying, "Well, let's find out." Satisfactory responses can be followed by, "That's right and that's what our story is about."*)

In our Bible story for today, Jesus asked his disciples, "What are people saying about me?" The disciples answered, "Some say you are John the Baptist. Others say you are a prophet." Then Jesus asked the disciples what they thought. The disciple named Peter gave Jesus the right answer.

If Jesus were to ask you, "Who am I?", what would you say? (*Wait for answers. They will probably say Jesus or Jesus Christ.*) Jesus is someone who loves people. You might remember the story when Jesus took one little boy's lunch of just five loaves of bread and two fish and he made five thousand lunches out of it to feed the people who had come to listen to him.

The Bible tells us that Jesus is the one who died on the cross to forgive our sins. The Bible says that three days later Jesus rose from the dead. He did that to show us that he has great power and can forgive our sins.

Now let's look at my name badge again. Here is my name, and

the cross means that I am a follower of Jesus. The cross lets you know that I love Jesus.

Today I have a special name badge for each of you. After we print your name on it, the badge will tell us something more than just your name. It will remind someone who sees you that you too love Jesus. When someone asks, "Who are you?", now you can not only tell them your name, but you can show them the cross and say, "I am someone who loves Jesus." (*If possible, have helpers available to print names on the badges. Otherwise just give each child a badge.*)

—P.F.

Sixth Sunday after Pentecost
———————————— • ————————————

The Gospel: Luke 9:51-62

Focus: Jesus invites us to follow him.

Experience: A trip through the sanctuary will remind the children of what it takes to follow Jesus.

Preparation: Map out in your mind the course for your trip through the sanctuary. You will want to begin at the baptismal font, visit the altar, altar railing, lectern, pulpit, and choir area, (also the organ if it is easy to reach) and return to the front of the church. Make a large map of your route. Optional: Makes copies of the map for the children.

Follow Me

Today we are going to go on a trip. Who would like to come along? Our trip won't take you very far from Mom or Dad, so you won't get homesick. I don't think we will get lost, but just in case, I have a map. (*If you made copies, distribute them. Otherwise, hold up your large one.*)

In our Bible lesson for today Jesus invited people to follow him. They said, "We can't! We are too busy today!" They didn't follow Jesus.

Well, Jesus also asks us to follow him. Saying we are too busy isn't a good excuse. This map will remind us in what ways we follow Jesus right here in worship. Look at the map and tell me where we go from here? (*Wait for answers.*)

Follow me! When we follow Jesus, we begin at the baptismal font. That's where your life with Jesus began. That's where you first began to know Jesus. Some of you have seen a baptism. What happens when someone is baptized? (*Wait for answers.*)

Now where do we go from here? Follow me! (*Lead children to altar.*) Does anyone know what this is called? (*Responses.*) It is an altar. Pastors often stand at the altar when they lead us in worship. It is a special table, isn't it? When we follow Jesus, we need to remember to worship. What do we do when we worship God? (*Sing, listen to the Bible and sermons, etc. Their answers might relate to the other areas you will visit.*)

It's time to get going. Where do we go from here? (*Walk to altar railing.*) We didn't have to go very far, did we? What is this called? (*Responses.*) What do we do here? This is where we celebrate communion. This is where we are reminded again and again that Jesus forgives us.

I know where we are going next. Follow me! (*Take them to the lectern.*) Here is where someone reads to us from the Bible. The Bible tells us how much God loves us.

Now, what is next? (*Take them to the pulpit.*) Does anyone know what this is called? (*Responses.*) It is a pulpit. What happens here? This is where the pastor talks about God's Word. When we follow Jesus, we have to remember what Jesus has said to us in the Bible. (*You may want to show the children the organ if it is accessible.*)

I think we have only one more place to visit. Can anyone find it on the map? Can anyone show us where it is? (*Let a child lead you to the choir area.*) What happens here? The choir sings, don't they? Some of you are in a choir. We hear God's Word from the lectern and pulpit, but we also hear it through the songs that are sung from right here. (*You might ask the children to thank the choir for being there.*) It looks to me like we need to get back to where we began. Who can help us get back? (*Responses.*)

That was quite a trip. You followed me so well. Some of you are very good at reading a map. As followers of Jesus, we need to remember all of those places. Jesus said to us, "Don't make excuses. Just come and follow me." When we visit the baptismal font, the altar, the altar railing, the lectern, the pulpit, and the choir area, we are following Jesus. Thanks for going on the trip with me this morning.   **—P.F.**

Seventh Sunday after Pentecost
—————————————————— • ——————————————————

The Gospel: Luke 10:1-12, 16, (17-20)

Focus: Following Jesus takes a willing heart.

Experience: Through conversation about what we carry in a suitcase, the children will be reminded that the call to follow Jesus does not demand large amounts of equipment but rather asks us to obey God's Word.

Preparation: Bring a large suitcase or backpack filled with a pair of shoes, a purse or wallet, and a Bible.

Baggage

(*As you carry the suitcase or backpack, act as if you have a very heavy load.*)
How many of you have ever gone on a trip? Tell me, where have you gone? (*Responses.*) When you go on a trip, what do you put in your suitcase? (*Responses.*)

In our Bible story, Jesus sent people out to different places. Their job was to tell others about Jesus and his love. Jesus told them, "Take only a few things along."

(*Look into your suitcase or backpack.*) I guess I have too much. (*Pull out a pair of shoes.*) I already have shoes, so I guess I don't need these.

(*Pull out a purse or wallet.*) I already have a purse or wallet, so I guess I don't need this.

Jesus reminds us that when we follow him, we don't need a lot of extra things. Let me see what I have left in my suitcase. Who wants to reach in and find out? (*A child pulls out the Bible.*) What is it? That's right. It's a Bible. It is God's Word. The Bible is filled with stories of Jesus. It tells us how to follow him.

When we follow Jesus, all we really need is his Word. We are not alone. (*Point toward the congregation.*) All of these other people are helping us on the trip. There are Sunday school teachers and parents and choir directors and lots of people who pray for us as we follow Jesus.

When I want to tell someone about Jesus, I won't need these extra shoes or an extra purse (wallet). All I need is what is in this book—God's Word—and the help of all of those people sitting out there. Those are the only things I need.   **—P.F.**

Eighth Sunday after Pentecost
———————————— • ————————————

The Gospel: Luke 10:25-37

Focus: The questions, "Who is my neighbor?" and "Who should I help?" are as important now as they were in Jesus' day.

Experience: The children will think about helping someone who is different from themselves, or someone they do not know.

Preparation: Bring a phone.

My Neighbor Who Doesn't Live Next Door

(*Place the phone somewhere close to you.*)

Let's pretend that someone you know gets hurt. Let's say it is a next-door neighbor, perhaps the dad of a friend of yours. He has fallen off the roof of his house. There he is, lying on the ground. (*Use your hands to gesture that he is lying in front of you.*) Someone needs to get to a phone. It might even be you if there isn't anyone else around. (*Hand the phone to a child.*) You call 9-1-1 (or the number that is appropriate for your community) and soon an ambulance arrives to take your neighbor to the hospital. It certainly is good that we have telephones to call and get help. It's so easy. (*Put the phone near you again to avoid distraction as you continue.*)

A long time ago when Jesus told his story about the Good Samaritan, there weren't any phones. A man was lying by the side of the road (*use same gesture*), robbed and beaten. Nearly dead. And he was a stranger in that area. He was a man the Good Samaritan had never met before, yet the Good Samaritan was willing to help him. What would you do? (*Allow responses.*) Let's pretend that you are a grown-up. There are no phones, no ambulances to call, and there in front of you is a man who is hurt and bleeding. If you're going to help him, you will have to do it yourself. He isn't a friend. He isn't a next-door neighbor. He's a stranger. Someone you don't know. Someone you aren't sure if you can trust. Is he worth the time? Should you spend hundreds of dollars to get him to a hospital and to pay his bills? You're a busy person. You have things to do, a family who needs you. You have more important matters to attend to.

Or do you? Jesus said the most important commandment for us to keep is to love God with all our heart and to love the stranger who needs our help. Jesus wants us to be good neighbors, to be kind to everyone, even if they don't live next door to us. — **R.J.C.**

Ninth Sunday after Pentecost

——————————————• ——————————————

The Gospel: Luke 10:38-42

Focus: We need to be still in order to listen.

Experience: The children will learn that being still helps them listen to the reading of God's Word.

Preparation: A megaphone made out of paper. (An alternative is to begin with a picture of Dumbo, the elephant with the big ears).

Mary the Listener

(Hold the lectern Bible in front of the children and with reverence open it to Luke 10. While tracing around the outer edge with your index finger, say, "This is the Word of God, and today we hear the story of Mary and Martha".*) (Hold up megaphone.)* Most of us don't need something like this in order to hear better. *(Demonstrate how the megaphone can be reversed in order to better capture the sound, or show a picture of Dumbo with his big ears.)* Today we will learn about a woman who really *wanted to hear* what Jesus said.

One day Jesus came to the home of Mary and Martha. Martha quickly got busy with serving Jesus while Mary sat at Jesus' feet and listened to his teachings. Of the two, Martha or Mary, who did the better thing? *(Responses.)*

The Bible says that Mary did because she stopped everything else and sat still so that she could *hear* what Jesus wanted to say to here. It was as if Mary held up to her ear this megaphone (or could hear as well as Dumbo). She really wanted to hear Jesus.

You have that very same opportunity to hear what Jesus wants to say to you. It can happen anytime and anyplace when you stop doing everything else and you become still enough to hear Jesus speaking. We have a very special book. *(Pick up a Bible.)* When we read from it, we should stop everything we are doing and listen as if Jesus himself had come to our house and wanted to talk with us.

"Dear God, we ask that we would be more like Mary—eager to hear the words of Jesus speaking to us. Help us to be still and listen with both ears. Amen."   **—R.J.C.**

Tenth Sunday after Pentecost
———————————— • ————————————

The Gospel: Luke 11:1-13

Focus: God wants to give good things to those who ask.

Experience: The children will talk about some of the many good gifts of God.

Preparation: Bring a crèche or figure of baby Jesus and a cross. (Place them in a box or bag.)

God Loves to Give Good Gifts

(*Hold the lectern Bible in front of the children and with reverence open it to Luke 11. While tracing around the outer edge with your index finger, say,* "This is the Word of God, and today we discover how much God loves to give us such good gifts."

God is very good to us. Sometimes we don't realize how many gifts we have received from God. Today we are going to talk about at least a few of them.

(*Open your bag or box and take out the crèche or baby Jesus.*) This is the best gift God ever gave us. Who is this baby? (*Jesus.*) What do we call the day that he was born? We celebrate it every December. (*Christmas.*) Jesus is the best gift. He is our Savior. (*Pull out the cross.*) What is this? (*A cross.*) Yes, Jesus died on the cross for us and forgives us all our sins. He became alive again on Easter. Jesus is our very best gift from God.

But God keeps giving us many good gifts every day—food and other things we need. How about clothing? I see all of you have nice clothes on today. Wow, isn't it great that God gives us food and clothes and places to live and so much more. How about parents and grandparents and friends? God must really love us a lot to give us so many good gifts!

God gave us the most important gift, Jesus, but God also gives us many, many other good gifts every day all through our lives.

"Thank you, God, for loving us so much that you sent your Son, Jesus, to be our Savior. Thank you, too, for all the good gifts you keep giving us—food to eat, clothes to wear, family and friends, and so many other gifts that we couldn't count all of them even if we tried. Amen."   **—R.J.C.**

Eleventh Sunday after Pentecost
————————————•————————————

The Gospel: Luke 12:13-21

Focus: Being rich in God is more important than being rich in toys.

Experience: The children will recall that a toy they once wanted so much is now rusted or broken or forgotten.

Preparation: Bring a broken or disregarded Christmas toy.

How Do I Want to Be Rich?

(Hold the lectern Bible in front of the children and with reverence open it to Luke 12. While tracing around the outer edge with your index finger, say, "This is the Word of God, and today we learn how to be truly rich."

Remember when Christmas was only a few weeks away? You had a list of things you wanted, and on that list there were one or two things you wanted very, very much. What were a few of those things? *(Entertain responses.)*

Try to remember the Christmas before that when you also had a list of things you wanted very, very much. Who can remember what some of those things were? *(Entertain responses.)* And who can remember other Christmases before that and what you thought you really had to have? *(Entertain responses.)*

(Bring out your broken or rusted toy.) A few years ago, this looked very nice, but look at it now. Toys come and go, and sometimes the ones we wanted don't matter much after a while.

A lot of us would like to grow up and be rich. We think that when we are rich, we can buy ourselves lots of toys, expensive grown-up toys like cars or boats or CDs or computers. Maybe they won't get broken or rust as quickly as this _____ *(name of toy).* But sooner or later they will. And all the time we are trying so hard to be rich, we may forget about God. We may think we don't have time to go to church on Sunday or to pray or to read the Bible. We would be so busy shopping that we wouldn't have time to help a stranger who is hurting.

As you grow up, you will need to make choices between wanting more and more toys and things and money, and wanting to worship and obey God. We need to be sure we don't forget God.

We will always want a few toys, and that's OK, but God is more important than having lots of toys and things.

"Dear God, there are so many things we want. We could make a long, long list. And yet we can be so much happier when we want you more than anything else. Amen." —**R.J.C.**

Twelfth Sunday after Pentecost

—————————— • ——————————

The Gospel: Luke 12:32-40

Focus: What we treasure most is safe in our hearts, where no thief can break in.

Experience: The children will think about their treasures and see that many of those treasures cannot be stolen from them.

Preparation: Bring a treasure box or jewelry box with a lock.

A Safe Place for My Treasures

(*Show the children the treasure box or jewelry box you brought.*) What did I bring today? (*Listen to responses. Elaborate if needed.*) Usually this box has valuable things in it, but today it happens to be empty. (*Show the children.*)

What kind of treasures do people have today? What kinds of things do they keep in locked boxes or safe places? (*Responses will probably include jewelry and money.*) People are often afraid that robbers or thieves might steal some of the things they think are valuable—maybe their TVs or cars. We all have things we don't want anyone to steal. What do you have that you wouldn't want anybody to steal? (*Responses will probably include toys, bikes, and related items.*)

Those are all treasures to us, but did you know that you have other treasures that *nobody* can steal? That is good news, isn't it? Those treasures are what we have in our hearts. We love other people like Mom and Dad, and nobody can steal that love out of our hearts. It is safe.

How about happiness? That is in our hearts. That happiness may have come because we have many good memories. Maybe we remember Christmases or birthdays or other happy events that have happened. No thief can ever steal those memories! What are some happy things you remember? (*Responses.*)

Best of all, we know that Jesus loves us, and we feel that love in our hearts. No thief can ever take Jesus' love away from us. So we do have quite a few treasures that are safe from thieves, safe in our hearts, don't we? (*Yes.*)

"God, we thank you that we have so many treasures that are safe from thieves because they are in our hearts. Thank you for all the love we feel, especially Jesus' love for us. In Jesus' name we pray, Amen."   **—R.J.C.**

Thirteenth Sunday after Pentecost
— • —

The Gospel: Luke 12:49-53

Focus: To do one thing well, we need to concentrate on it. Christians concentrate on following Jesus.

Experience: The children will be asked to do several activities at once, such as balancing a book on their head, chewing gum, and jumping up and down. By doing only one activity at a time, children will experience the importance of concentrating, focusing, and being single-minded. (Depending on the number of children present, all children can participate in all or some of the activities. Or two can perform the multiple balancing act and several the single balancing act.)

Preparation: Bring a couple of balls; chewing gum; some small boards, books, pieces of cardboard, wooden blocks, or other things that can be balanced on a child's head.

Doing Too Many Things at Once

Good morning, children. I am very happy to see you. Is anybody here for the first time? (*If so, introduce yourself and welcome the child or children.*) I am glad that you are here.

Today I would like to see how good you are at balancing things on your head. Take one of these (*pass out boards, blocks, books, etc.*), stand up, and balance what I give you on your head. Go ahead. (*Let children do it.*) You all are quite good.

Now, I would like to see how good you are at balancing something on your head while chewing gum. (*Distribute the gum. Let the children chew and balance.*) It is a little tougher, isn't it? But you seem to be doing all right.

This time, I want you to keep on chewing gum and balancing the object on your head, but now walk around. Go ahead. Let me see how well you can do. (*Let the children do it.*)

It is getting tougher. Some of you are having a rough time. Doing all three things at the same time is difficult.

Now, I want you to stop walking around. Keeping chewing your gum, keep balancing those objects on your heads, but also jump up and down or try to catch a ball. Go ahead. (*Let them do it.*

Most likely, the children won't be able to keep balancing the items on their heads.) Whoa, you are losing those objects you put on your heads! Try again and try harder. Jump up and down or toss a ball *and* keep balancing the objects on your head. And don't forget to chew your gum. (*Let them try again.*)

It is almost impossible, isn't it? It is quite easy to do one thing at a time. But to do two or more things at the same time is nearly impossible. To keep those objects from falling from our heads, we have to pay attention to balancing them, and we can't walk around a lot or jump up and down or catch a ball. To do one thing right, we have to concentrate on doing it.

The same is true about trying to be like Jesus. In order to be a good follower of Jesus, we have to concentrate, give it our best effort, and try to be loving and kind like him. We need to avoid doing things, like fighting and getting even. Jesus is our focus.

—N.F.H.

Fourteenth Sunday after Pentecost
———————————————•———————————————

The Gospel: Luke 13:22-30

Focus: How do we get into heaven? Not through works or tools but through faith in Jesus Christ.

Experience: The children will see how particular objects are linked with particular tasks and results, and they will hear how faith in Jesus is linked with getting into heaven.

Preparing: Bring a credit card or ATM card, some tools, money, keys, and a picture of Jesus or a Bible. Put them in a bag or box so that the children can only see the object you take out.

How Do We Get into Heaven?

Good morning, children. I am very happy to see you here this morning. Is anyone here for the first time? (*If so, introduce yourself and welcome the child or children.*)

Today, I brought a bunch of stuff, and I would like to see if you know what each of the items is used for. (*Reach for one of the tools.*) Do you know what this can be used for? (*Let the children respond. Discourage incorrect ideas, but explain why.*) OK, those are some good suggestions. (*Reach for the next object, maybe another tool*). And what is the best use for this? (*Again, let the children respond and affirm their answers. Correct them as needed. Follow the same procedure with the remaining objects—except for the picture of Jesus or Bible.*)

Most of your suggestions are great. You are very smart children. But now I have another question. (*Pick up each object and ask the following question.*) Can I use this to get into heaven? (*The children should respond with "no." If they are indecisive, you may remind them of the item's uses they determined earlier.*) No, we can't get into heaven with this.

Oh, here is one more item, I overlooked it earlier. (*Pull out the picture of Jesus or a Bible.*) Can this help us get into heaven? (*Wait for responses.*) Yes, Jesus—the person in this picture, the person who died on a cross, the person about whom we learn in the Bible—he can help us get into heaven. We can trust Jesus to forgive our sins. Jesus is our Savior. He is our way into heaven.   **—N.F.H.**

Fifteenth Sunday after Pentecost
—————————————•—————————————

The Gospel: Luke 14:1, 7-14

Focus: Hospitality is making a visitor feel welcome.

Experience: The children will be asked to extend hospitality by hugging and welcoming a stuffed animal that is visiting the worship service for the first time.

Preparation: Bring one or more stuffed animals, preferably one(s) that the children have never seen before. Wrap it in a small blanket before you come.

Welcoming a Visitor

Good morning, children. Is anyone here for the first time? (*If so, introduce yourself and welcome the child or children.*) I am very happy that you are here.

There is somebody else visiting us today. (*Take the blanket off the stuffed animal.*) Does anyone know who this is? Well, you probably don't know her because she is very new. She came to my house yesterday to talk. Her name is Chris. I invited her to come to worship with me today. Chris had never been to worship or church before, so she was a bit afraid and shy. Chris is shy and afraid because she looks different from you, because Chris has no money, no parents, no friends.

But I told Chris that you are a very friendly group of children and that you will like her and love her and make her feel welcome.

How can we make Chris feel loved and welcome here? (*Wait for responses. Affirm the good ones. Implement the good ones—like "We can say good morning to Chris," or "We can tell Chris that we love her" or "One of us can sit with Chris," etc. If one of the children suggests giving Chris a hug, affirm the response and say that you will come back to it. After the children run out of ideas, go back to the hugging idea. If no one brings it up, ask the children if each one of them is willing to give Chris a hug. Assist the children in passing Chris from one person to the next. Encourage them to be gentle, to avoid roughness.*)

Those are some very good ideas. I would like to suggest that each one of you give Chris a hug. And if you feel like it, tell Chris, "I am glad you're here" or something like that.

(*While the children are hugging Chris, say,*) You are a wonderful group of children. What you are doing right now is making someone who is very different from you feel loved and welcome. And that is exactly what Jesus wants us to do. Thanks so much for doing that for Chris.   **—N.F.H.**

Sixteenth Sunday after Pentecost
——————————————————•——————————————————

The Gospel: Luke 14:25-33

Focus: The cost of being a follower of Jesus includes helping to get things done that need to get done inside and outside the church.

Experience: The children will spend most of the sermon time on a project that needs to be done either around the church or for members or others in need. Through this the children will experience (a) discipleship and (b) its cost because they have to give up their special time in worship.

Preparation: Think of, and if necessary prepare, a project that the children can do during the time usually allotted to the children's sermon, such as cleaning up a mess, straightening out books, sharpening pencils, writing a note or drawing a picture for shut-ins or hospitalized persons, or some related tasks.

Followers of Jesus

Good morning, children. It is great to see you this morning. Is anyone here for the first time? (*If so, introduce yourself and welcome the child or children.*) I am very happy that you are here.

You and I and all the people here are followers of Jesus. We love him, and he loves us. We try to live the way Jesus lived and try to do things he wants us to do. What do you think Jesus would want us to do at home, with our friends, and here at church? (*Responses may include being kind, doing what our parents ask us to do, not fighting, doing nice things for others, praying, coming to church and Sunday school, and so forth.*)

Sometimes it is easy for us to be followers of Jesus, but sometimes it is hard. Sometimes followers of Jesus have to do some work when we would rather do something else. Even though we know Jesus loves us just the way we are, whether we are willing to work or not, we know that he likes us to be helpful.

Your parents and other grown-ups help a lot in our church. They teach Sunday school, they are ushers, they help keep the church clean, they _____ . (*Name other tasks.*) They also do many good things for other people outside the church every day at work or at home or wherever they are. They know that followers of Jesus need to help out when things need to be done. And guess what! Followers of Jesus who are young, like you children, sometimes are asked to help with projects for people inside or outside the church. This morning I need your help. I need you to help me _____. (*Tell the children what task(s) you have chosen.*) So let's stop our children's time a little early and go do the job. (*Explain the job, give instructions, lead the children there, and let them do it. After they have finished, thank them.*) Thank you, children. You are willing to help with things that need to be done. You are good followers of Jesus!

—N.F.H.

Seventeenth Sunday after Pentecost
———————————————— • ————————————————

The Gospel: Luke 15:1-10

Focus: The Gospel tells about Jesus, the good shepherd. Every person is so important that, like Jesus, we will try to reach out to each one if he or she is in need or lost or missing.

Experience: Like the shepherd in the parable, the children will stop what they are doing to seek and find someone who is missing. One child who attends regularly will pretend to be missing today and will hide somewhere, preferably nearby, perhaps under a coat in a pew or in a corner behind something.

Preparation: Instruct one child and his or her parents about what you need the child to do. It would be especially good if a sibling could point out during the sermon that his or her brother (sister) is missing.

When Someone Is Lost

Good morning, children, I am so glad to see you. Is anyone here for the first time? (*If so, introduce yourself and welcome the child or children.*) It is nice to have you all here.

Today, I feel like counting you. Can you help me count? (*Let the children count or help with the counting.*) Now, do you know of any boy or girl who normally comes but isn't here today? (*Wait for responses. During this time, the child who has been instructed ahead should report the brother or sister missing from the children's time.*) You are right. _____ (*name*) is missing. But I thought she (he) was here today. I thought I saw _____ (*name*) earlier. She (he) came with you, didn't she (he)? (*If you are discussing a missing friend, say,*) You talked with _____ (*name*) before the service, didn't you?

Did _____ (*name*) leave? Let's ask her (his) mom or her dad. (*Do that if possible.*) No, _____ (*name*) did not leave. So she (he) must be somewhere here in the building. What shall we do? Let's do what Jesus would do. In today's Gospel lesson he tells us about a shepherd looking for a sheep that is missing and about a woman looking for a lost coin. Jesus says that's how he feels about us. Each one of us is so important to him that he will come to us when we are lost or in need. And since each one of us is so important to

God, we can show others that they are important to us. So let's try to find _____ (*name*). (*Go with the children and look for the missing child. When you find the child, bring him or her back with you and talk to the congregation.*) Look, we found _____ (*name*)! We are so happy. The one who was lost has been found. **—N.F.H.**

Eighteenth Sunday after Pentecost
————————————— • —————————————

The Gospel: Luke 16:1-13

Focus: No one can serve two masters. We cannot serve God and wealth.

Experience: The children will play a variation of the game Simon Says. Two adults give instructions to the children. First, they take turns giving commands. Then they give the same command in unison. Finally, they give conflicting instructions at the same time or one shortly after the other.

Preparation: Recruit an adult of the opposite gender to help you. Give that person a list of the following commands and instructions: (*You may add others of your own.*)

1. Instructions spoken by one person at a time, taking turns:
   "Simon says, Close your eyes!"
   "Simone says, Open your eyes!"
   "Simon says, Clap your hands once!"
   "Simone says, Clap your hands two times!"

2. Instructions spoken by both persons in unison:
   "Simon (Simone) says, Shake your head!"
   "Simon says, Stand up!"
   "Simon (Simone) says, Say good morning!"

3. Instructions spoken so that the second one comes right after the first one is finished and the children do not have enough time to implement it, creating conflicting instructions:
   "Simon says, Raise your hands into the air above your head!"
   "Simone says, Touch your knees with your hands!"
   "Simon says, Say your name out loud ten times!"
   "Simone says, Be very, very quiet!"
   "Simon says, Sit down on the floor!"
   "Simone says, Stand on one foot!"

Practice ahead of time so that in the third part the children will hear two conflicting commands and be stumped by them.

Simon Says

Good morning, children. It is wonderful to see you. Is anyone here for the first time? *If so, introduce yourself and welcome the child or children.)* I am glad all of you are here.

I have asked _____ (*name*) to help us today with the children's time. We are going to play a game most of you know: Simon Says. _____ (*name*) and I will take turns. (*Have the male leader say,* "I'll be Simon," *and have the female leader say,* "I'll be Simone.") Please listen carefully to what Simon or Simone says: It does not matter whether it is _____ (*name*) or I who is speaking. Do you remember how to play? When you hear "Simon says" or "Simone says," you follow the instructions. Just listen carefully and play along. OK? Thanks.

(*Do the Simon Says instructions listed above under #1.)* OK, that went quite well. Now let's try something a little different. Again, listen carefully and do what Simon says. (*Do sequence #2.)* All right, now we are having fun. You all are doing a great job. Let's keep going. (*Do sequence #3.)* Whoa, what is the matter? What is going on? Looks like you all are a bit confused? Is it difficult to do what Simon and Simone say? (*If it is not, you may want to try segment three again, paying attention that each instruction is clearly heard and that they come quickly, one after the other. The children may now be more alert to a shift in the game, while they may have simply overheard or ignored the second command in the previous round.)*

OK, let's stop. Somehow it was harder for you to do what we said during this last round. You all were doing fine earlier when we took turns giving instructions or said them together. What seems to be the problem? (*Await answers. The children should refer to the conflicting commands coming close together. If they don't, you may have to point it out.)* Yes, when _____ (*name*) and I gave you different instructions at almost the same time, the game became very difficult. And it probably wasn't as much fun. It is impossible to follow two different instructions at the same time. Jesus knew that too. He said it in today's Gospel lesson: "No one can serve two masters." So we as Christians always need to put Jesus first. Otherwise our lives become as mixed up and complicated as our game of Simon Says just became.

The only way to play the game right is for only one person to give instructions. Right? OK, that's what we will do. (*Repeat sequence #3 but take turns.)* The right way to live as Christians is to follow the instructions that Jesus gives us. Thank you, children. **—N.F.H.**

Nineteenth Sunday after Pentecost
———————————————— • ————————————————

The Gospel: Luke 16:19-31

Focus: God communicates love to us through Jesus. We communicate it to others.

Experience: The children will communicate God's love and their love to someone who is not at worship (such as shut-ins or hospitalized people) by drawing pictures for them.

Preparation: Bring plenty of paper and marker pens or crayons (so that the children can draw a picture), stamped envelopes (parents are more likely to mail them that way), and index cards with the address(es) of the person(s) to whom the pictures will be sent. You may wish to ask some adults or youth to help get the children started on their pictures.

One Way to Show Love

Good morning, children. I am very glad to see you all this morning. Is anyone here for the first time? (*If so, introduce yourself and welcome the child or children.*)

I need your help this morning. I need some ideas from you about how I can tell my mom (*or another relative*) that I love her a whole lot. How can I let her know? (*Wait for and affirm responses*). Those are all great ideas. Do you have any others? (*Wait.*) Thanks for your ideas.

Now, I need your help again. I need you to let some people know that God loves them. There are some in our congregation who cannot come to church. (*You may mention the names of your congregation's hospitalized persons, even show the children their pictures if you have a picture directory.*) We need to remind them that God loves them. I brought enough paper and marker pens (crayons) as well as envelopes for each of you. (*Distribute.*) Let's all draw pictures of flowers or something colorful for these friends who can't come to church. Then I want you to put your picture into the envelope. Ask your mom or dad to help you copy the address from this index card (*give one to each child*) onto the envelope and mail it.

Let's take a minute to get started on this project. I will draw a picture, too. Go ahead and get started. (*Take a minute or two to get the children going on their project. If other adults are assisting, they can encourage or help some of the children get started.*) You can finish these later.

Thank you so very, very much. The Bible tells us that God loves us. And we learn about Jesus' love for us in Sunday school and in worship. That is good news. Today we are passing along the good news to others who cannot be here to hear it. Thanks for helping.

—N.F.H.

Twentieth Sunday after Pentecost
————————————— • —————————————

The Gospel: Luke 17:1-10

Focus: The Gospel lesson talks about repentance and forgiveness.

Experience: The children will ask for forgiveness and will forgive in three languages.

Preparation: Write each of the following sentences on a large piece of paper or tagboard. The first statement goes on one side, the second (the pronunciation guide) goes on the back. If you don't speak these languages, and you know someone who does, ask that person to help you pronounce the sentences properly. Or ask that person to actually participate during the children's time. If you are fluent in additional languages, you may use those languages instead of, or in addition to, the ones used here.

(German) *"Es tut mir leid vergib mir."* (*Is toot mea lite. Fergeeb mea.*)

(French) *"Je suis fâché. Faitez grâce de moi."* (Zhuh swee fahshay. Fett grahs deh mwah.)

(English) "I am sorry. Forgive me."

(German) *"Ja. Ich vergebe dir."* (Yah. Ick fergehbe deer.)

(French) *"Oui. Je fais grâce de toi."* (Wee. Zhuh fay grahs deh twah.)

(English) "Yes, I forgive you."

Asking for Forgiveness

Good morning, children. It is very good to have you here this morning. Is anyone here for the first time? (*If so, introduce yourself and welcome the child or children.*)

Today, I want to teach you a few short sentences in some other languages. I have written each short sentence on a piece of paper (tagboard, posterboard). The languages are German and French. Each one says something about being sorry and asking for forgiveness.

First, the German sentence. Listen to me a couple of times. Then repeat each word after me. Then say the whole sentence. (*Hold up the card with the first German phrase. Say the phrase twice, slowly and clearly. Then say one word at a time, allowing time for the children to repeat each one. Then say the whole phrase with the children.)* That was very good. *(If it was not good, repeat the previous step. Follow the same procedure with the French phrase.)*

Now, the third one is really easy. Repeat after me. "I am sorry. Please forgive me." Great job. That was pretty easy, wasn't it? After all, it is our language, English. And it means the same thing as the other sentences that we just practiced. Do you remember how to say "I am sorry. Please forgive me" in German? *(Let them answer. Hold the card up and encourage the children if necessary.)* And in French? *(Follow the same procedure.)* Good job!

Now you have said, "I am sorry. Please forgive me" in three languages. That is very good.

But what do you say to the person if someone says to *you*, "I am sorry. Please forgive me"? *(Wait for answers.)* Right, we might say something as simple as "Yes, I forgive you." In today's Gospel lesson Jesus asks us to forgive when someone asks for forgiveness.

So, we know to give the right answer in English: Yes, I forgive you. Let's practice the right answer in the other languages that we just learned. If someone comes to you and says in German, "*Es tut mir leid. Vergib mir,*" we would say, "*Ja. Ich vergebe dir.*" *(Hold up the correct card and practice the answer with the children. Then do the same thing in French.)*

You are very good learners. Now all of us know how to ask for forgiveness in three languages, and we know how to forgive someone else in those three languages. Thanks.   **—N.F.H.**

Twenty-first Sunday after Pentecost
———————————————— • ————————————————

The Gospel: Luke 17:11-19

Focus: Jesus, the healer, told the leper, "Your faith has made you well."

Experience: The children will be asked to pretend to have an illness, injury, or pain and will experience the words spoken by Jesus which heals their pretend-illnesses.

Preparation: Make a list of injuries, illnesses, or pains that can be easily acted out in pantomime, such as a broken or sprained leg, being blind, or having pain in a jaw, arm, leg, head, or stomach. Write them or draw them on index cards which you will give to each child. You may want to ask adults to assist, or you may want to think ahead about pairing each younger child with an older one so that younger children have some help in acting out their illness or injury. If you have a large number of children, ask several children to pantomime the same illness or pain.

Your Faith Has Made You Well

Hello, children! I am very happy to see you. Is there anyone here today who is with us for the first time? (*If so, introduce yourself and welcome the child or children.*) It is good to have each of you here today.

Today, we are going to do pantomime. Pantomime means acting our something without using your voice. Let me give you an example. (*Pretend to play the guitar and sing.*) Of course, you knew what I was pretending to do. I was pantomiming a musician playing the guitar and singing.

But I want you to pantomime or act out having an illness or an injury. Each one of you will get a card with the word or picture of an illness, ache, or injury on it. I would like you older children to pair up with someone younger. (*Give directions and make arrangements.*) OK, here are your cards. (*Distribute.*) Take a minute to think about how to pantomime that illness, pain, or injury, and then practice. Then we will try to guess what everyone is pantomiming. (*Give them time to practice.*)

OK, now let's see if we can guess what everyone is pantomiming. (*Give each child or group of children a chance to perform. Let the others guess.*) Good. Nicely done.

Now, we have only *pretended* to have an illness or ache. In today's Gospel lesson we hear about some people who had a real illness. They were called lepers because they had an illness called leprosy. They came to Jesus and believed that he could heal them. And he did! Jesus said, "Your faith has made you well." Jesus can help us get well from all kinds of illnesses, pains, and aches.

Let's pantomime our pretend-illnesses again. When I say, "Jesus says, 'Your faith has made you well,' " I want you to pretend that you are well, that you are no longer sick. How would you do that? How would you pantomime that? (*Listen to responses.*) Right, you would smile, look happy, perhaps wave your hands, walk around, and so forth. Let's do it. (*Proceed. With a large group, you may pronounce healing for several at once.*)

Thank you, children. You helped us see the difference Jesus can make. Jesus helps us get well from all kinds of illnesses and helps with all kinds of problems. We are very thankful. **—N.F.H.**

Twenty-second Sunday after Pentecost
———————————————————— • ————————————————————

The Gospel: Luke 18:1-8a

Focus: Jesus told his followers "to pray always and not to lose heart." There are many ways to pray and many reasons to pray.

Experience: The children will talk about prayer and try several positions of prayer that are described in the Bible.

Preparation: Read these verses ahead of time, but do not read them to the children. Just mention them: Psalm 47:1 (clap hands), Psalm 134:2 (lift up hands), Psalm 149:3 (dance), Deuteronomy 9:18 (lie face down, prostrate), Ephesians 3:14 (kneel), Mark 11:25 (stand).

Jesus Invites Us to Pray

Today we are going to think about praying. Jesus wants us to pray about all kinds of things. What have you prayed about? (*Allow responses. Quite likely they will mention bedtime prayers to bless family members, prayers when they were in trouble or lost or when someone was sick, table prayers.*)

How do we hold our hands when we pray? (*You and the children can first fold hands with fingers flat, then with fingers intertwined.*) Did you know there are other ways that people pray? Let's find out some ways that people in the Bible prayed.

Psalm 47:1 says that people clapped their hands and shouted to God with songs of joy. Let's clap our hands and say "Alleluia," which means "Praise God." (*All clap several times and say "Alleluia."*) Psalm 134:2 says people lifted their hands and blessed the Lord. Let's do that. (*All lift up hands and say "Bless the Lord."*)

Psalm 149:3 says the people are to "praise his name with dancing." Let's dance around with our hands waving, and say "Praise the name of God!" Be careful not to run into each other. (*All dance around and say that phrase.*)

(*Optional, depending on space and preference.*) Deuteronomy 9:18 tells about Moses lying flat on the ground, face down, praying to God. Let's try that. (*All lie down and say "God, help me."*)

Next we will try what you already may have used at home or church or other places. In Ephesians 3:14 Paul writes, "I bow my knees before the Father." He kneeled. Let's try kneeling, and let's pray, "Thank you, God, for loving us." (*All kneel and pray that phrase.*) In Mark 11:25, it says, "Whenever you *stand* praying," so let's stand up, fold our hands, and I will lead us in a closing prayer.

"God, we know you want us to pray, and we can pray in many different ways. Help us to remember to pray when we are happy, when we have something to thank you for, when we are worried or sick, before we go to bed, and many other times. We thank you for everything, but especially for sending Jesus, our Savior." Let's all say Amen together. (*Amen!*)   **—M.C.A. and G.W.**

Twenty-third Sunday after Pentecost
——————————— • ———————————

The Gospel: Luke 18:9-14

Focus: God knows who we are (both good things and bad things) and still loves us. The person who comes before God without long lists of achievements will find out that God loves him or her anyway.

Experience: The children will experiment with a mirror to see how too much pride and attention to ourselves can come between us and God.

Preparation: Bring a mirror, preferably nine to twelve inches in height so that it virtually hides your face when you hold it up.

How God Sees Us

Who can tell me what this is? (*Show mirror.*) What do you see when you look into it? (*Pass the mirror around.*) Go ahead and look. What do you see? (*They will likely say, "Me!".*)

Now suppose I am talking to you, and I put the mirror between us. What happens? What do you see? Do you even see me at all? (*Hold mirror in front of your face. The children will answer that they can't see you very well.*) No, you can't see me, and I can only see myself. Would we be able to talk very well this way? (*No, it would be hard.*)

Now suppose I am praying to God. (*Maybe bow head or look up.*) What if I hold the mirror up like this. (*Again hold mirror in front of your face.*) What do I see? Am I thinking about God? (*No.*) You and I couldn't talk very well when I did this, and I can't talk to God very well either when I am just looking at myself.

Today's Gospel tells us about a man who only thought about how great he was, so when he prayed to God he only talked about himself. He didn't have a real mirror, but it was as though all he could see was his own face (*hold mirror up*). It was as though he was saying, "God, look at me. I'm better than everyone else."

The other man in this story knew he wasn't perfect, so he asked God to help him and forgive him. It was as though he put down the mirror between himself and God. (*Put mirror down.*)

When we pray to God, we know that God already knows all about us, both the good and the bad things. And God loves us

anyway. We can be honest with God when we pray, knowing we
are loved and forgiven.   **—M.C.A. and G.W.**

Twenty-fourth Sunday after Pentecost

———————————— • ————————————

The Gospel: Luke 19:1-10

Focus: God can change the heart. Jesus' acceptance of Zacchaeus transformed him from an uncaring person to one who cared very much and wanted to treat people right.

Experience: The children will experience having money taken from them as they hear about selfish Zacchaeus, and they will get some money back after they hear about how Zacchaeus changed.

Preparation: Bring enough pennies to give three to every child plus some extras that you will put in the collection plate. Also bring a collection plate to where you will be speaking to the children.

Change of Heart

Today we are going to play a game to figure out how Zacchaeus, a person whom nobody liked, turned into a person everybody liked. Suppose you had this much money. (*Give every child two pennies.*) Now suppose I was the tax collector and I came and took money from you, one penny each. (*Take a penny from each.*) Do you like paying taxes? (*No.*) Well, neither did the people in Jesus' time. Now, what if I was a selfish tax collector and I made you give me another penny. (*Take the remaining penny from each.*) Would you like that very much? Would you like me very much? (*No.*) Of course you wouldn't.

What if there was a big parade in town. Have you ever been to a parade? Was it crowded? (*Listen to responses.*) We will have an imaginary parade. It is really crowded. I am that tax collector who takes too much money. I am a short person, and I want to get out in front. Will you let me through so I can see? (*No. We don't like you.*) How do you think I'd feel if nobody liked me and nobody helped me? (*Unhappy.*) Let's suppose there is a big tree here. I'll pretend to climb it so I can see the parade. (*Pretend to climb.*)

This is a special parade because Jesus is in it. In fact, the whole parade is for Jesus. Here he comes! And guess what. He stops by the tree, looks up, and sees me. He tells me he wants to come to my house to visit me! How do you suppose I feel? (*Happy.*)

Now we will stop our imaginary parade and talk about Zacchaeus. At first he was greedy and took people's money just like I took yours. But when Jesus came to his house, he changed completely. He gave back that money he took after he collected the taxes (*give each child a penny*) and then he gave them even more (*give each child two more pennies*) because he felt bad for cheating the people.

After that he gave half of the money he still had in order to help the poor. (*Put half of your extra pennies into the offering plate.*)

Do you know why Zacchaeus changed? (*Listen to responses.*) Jesus showed Zacchaeus he loved him. Jesus changed him with love. By showing Zacchaeus that he loved him, Jesus showed Zacchaeus that he was worth loving. When Zacchaeus knew that Jesus loved him, he wanted to do the right thing. He wanted to show love to others.

Jesus loves us, too, and that makes us want to be kind and to show love to other people as well. **—M.C.A. and G.W.**

Twenty-fifth Sunday after Pentecost
——————————— • ———————————

The Gospel: Luke 20:27-38

Focus: When we leave this earthly realm and live with God in heaven, our lives will be very different.

Experience: The children will talk about heaven.

What Is Heaven Like?

Today we are going to talk about heaven. Do people who are still alive go to heaven? (*No.*) Well, then when do they go to heaven? (*After they have died.*) So none of you has seen heaven, right? (*No, we haven't.*) No, of course not. We don't go to heaven until we die.

Do you know anyone who has gone to heaven and has come back to tell us what it is like? (*No.*) So we really do not know exactly what heaven will be like, do we?

How many of you have a pet, maybe a cat or dog? (*Listen to responses.*) Will we have pets in heaven? (*Listen to responses.*) We don't know for sure. I hope we do! How many of you have dark hair? light hair? red hair? (*Responses.*) Do we know how we will look in heaven, what color our hair will be? (*No.*) Maybe a grandpa who had gray hair when he died will get to have black hair in heaven, just like he did when he was younger. We don't really know. So, can we figure out what heaven will be from what it is like on earth? (*Responses.*) No, we can't.

But the good news is that we do know heaven will be wonderful. The Bible tells us some things about heaven. We will be with Jesus. We will feel great, and we will know we are loved. Jesus has told us that life in heaven will be very different from the way it is here now. Think about how many sad things happen now, like fights and wars, people getting shot by guns, car accidents. (*You may invite them to name some bad things that happen.*) But in heaven there will only be good things. We won't ever hurt again or cry again. We know heaven will be full of wonderful surprises for us. But for now God asks us to follow Jesus the best we can to make this world a good place for others. God wants us to show kindness and love to others whenever we can.   **—M.C.A. and G.W.**

Twenty-sixth Sunday after Pentecost
————————————— • —————————————

The Gospel: Luke 21:5-19

Focus: Jesus taught the importance of patience and endurance.

Experience: The children will think about things that take time and will learn how it feels to be patient.

Preparation: Bring along one of these (or some other) before-and-after pairs: flour and cookies, seeds and the vegetable or fruit (perhaps apples) they produce, milk and cheese. In each case, have the "after" item in a bag or out of sight. You may wish to bring enough of the "after" item (cookies, carrot sticks, etc.) to distribute to the children.

When We Have to Wait

Today we're going to talk about patience, how to be patient. Do you know what it means to be patient? (*Listen to responses and clarify. We are patient when we are willing to wait for something without complaining.*) Jesus told people that they should have patience even when bad things happen.

Let's see why patience is so important. Sometimes we really need to be patient. Look at what I brought along. (*Show them the flour, seeds, or whatever the first half of the before-and-after pair is*).

If you were hungry and wanted to eat, how would this (*show first item*) help you? (*Allow responses. Flour is difficult to eat. Seeds are unappetizing. Milk is OK.*) What if we took some time and got this as a result? (*Show "after" item: cookies, apple or other vegetable or fruit, cheese. Then listen to responses. Describe the process of transformation that takes place to get from the "before" item to the "after" item.*) Would that take awhile? (*Yes.*) What if you gave up, if you didn't have any patience? Would you ever get _____ (cookies out of flour, apples from seeds, etc.)? If you have patience, you eventually get what you are waiting for. What if something bad happened? (*Give an example appropriate to the item you brought, such as mice eating the cheese.*) Could you start all over again? (*Listen to responses.*) Of course you could. That is part of patience, too.

Jesus told his disciples that sometimes bad things would happen to them. Just because they were Christians didn't mean life would always be easy. In fact, sometimes it would be hard. He told them never to give up. Instead he said to have—what? (*Responses.*) That's right, have patience. And Jesus wants *us* to have patience, too.

(*As the children leave, you may wish to distribute cookies or apples or whatever your "after" item was.*)   **—M.C.A. and G.W.**

Twenty-seventh Sunday after Pentecost

—————————————— • ——————————————

The Gospel: Luke 19:11-27

Focus: God wants us to use our gifts wisely.

Experience: The children will hear about one of your skills and think of things they can do and enjoy doing.

Preparation: Bring along something you enjoy and are skilled at using, such as tools, a musical instrument, or sports equipment.

Using Our Gifts

Let's talk a little about things we like to do and things we do well. I brought this _____ today (*describe what you brought along*) because I really like to _____ . (*Describe when and what you play on the instrument, how and when you use the tools to build or cook or whatever. Be sure to include the fact that you are able to do this skill and that you enjoy doing it.*)

What are some of the things you children like to do and do well? (*Develop a conversation with several children. What can they do on a playground (swing, climb, play ball)? Can they build things with Legos™ or other construction toys? Can they sing, read, play an instrument? Are they friendly and helpful when they play with other children? Can they help with little brothers and sisters? Can they help Mom or Dad or grandparents? If time allows, you might also ask what their parents or grandparents are skilled at doing.*)

All these things we can do are gifts from God. God makes us able to _____ . (*Name some things mentioned: run, play, be friendly, help others, read, sing.*) The more you practice and do these things, the better you become at them.

God wants us to use all the gifts God has given to us, including the gift of being loving and kind. All our gifts from God make the world a better place. And God wants us to use our gifts and enjoy this beautiful world.   **—M.C.A. and G.W.**

Christ the King—Last Sunday after Pentecost

———————————————— • ————————————————

The Gospel: Luke 23:35-43

Focus: Jesus is King, but his kingdom is not based on might and physical power but on love and spiritual power.

Experience: The children will think about what kings usually do and learn about the kind of king Jesus is.

Preparation: Bring a map or globe if you wish.

Jesus, Our King

Today we are going to talk about kings. Suppose you lived in a kingdom (*with your finger, outline an area on a map or globe if you are using one*) and you were looking for a king. What would you want your king to be like? What would you want him to do? (*Allow responses and help children if needed. You may want to write some responses down because you will use a few later. Encourage ideas about physical power, such as having strong armies or powerful weapons.*) How should people treat their king? (*Responses.*) Where would the king live? (*Responses.*)

When Jesus lived on earth, people wanted him to be king. They wanted him to _____ . (*Recap some of their earlier responses: feed them, protect them, give them money, be powerful and have a big army so he could destroy enemies, etc.*) But Jesus was a different kind of king. He did not want to set up a rich and powerful kingdom on earth with big armies. That made some of the people really mad! They finally decided to kill him by hanging him on a cross, but before they did, they made fun of him. Do you remember the kind of crown they put on his head? (*crown of thorns*). They didn't understand what kind of a king he was.

Hardly anybody understood what kind of a king he was. A lot of the time even the disciples didn't realize it. But one person did— one of the men who was dying on a cross next to Jesus. He said to Jesus, "Remember me when you come into your kingdom."

Jesus said that this man would soon be with him in Paradise, which means heaven. This man knew Jesus had a different kind of kingdom.

Jesus does not rule over people with big armies or guns and bombs. Jesus is the King of love. He is the King who rules with love, and we love him in return. Jesus our King loves *us*, and *we* love Jesus our King!   **—M.C.A. and G.W.**